Aren't We Rich!

Lee R. McMurrin, Ph.D.

Copyright © 2015 Lee R. McMurrin

Cover and book design by Thomas Osborne

All rights reserved. No part of this book may be reproduced, stored in a retrieval system, or transmitted in any form, or by any means, electronic, mechanical, photocopying, recording or otherwise; without prior written permission of the author.

Library of Congress Control Number: 2015918063

ISBN: 978-0-692-56673-2

Printed in the United States of America

DEDICATION

*This book is dedicated
to the memory of my mother, Myrtle McMurrin,
for her devotion to Christian values,
and the eternal optimism she expressed
several times during the Great Depression.
Through the crises of the 1937 flood,
extreme poverty, the polio epidemic of 1944,
and two major wars (World War II and the
Korean War), she and her family
participated and survived.*

ACKNOWLEDGEMENTS

Several individuals who were members of the organization known as the Visiting Angels not only provided household services, but also took dictation and typed the script for the book. Particularly noteworthy are the contributions of Micki Bartlemay who, in her career, edited publications of large corporations, and applied her highly developed skills to repeatedly editing the book.

The greatest contribution to the book was the professional work of Louise Hawker, who was involved at every step, from the beginning to the publishing of the book. She added background information, edited the manuscript, arranged the pictures, and sought out Thomas Osborne. He took the copy of the book and prepared it for publication.

LEE R. MCMURRIN

Contents

CHAPTER 1
Introduction, 1

CHAPTER 2
Rich Experiences in Family Life, 5

CHAPTER 3
Rich Work Experiences in My Youth, 13

CHAPTER 4
Rich Experiences with Family—A Talented Wife as Homemaker, 17

CHAPTER 5
Rich Experiences in Music, 25

CHAPTER 6
Rich Experiences as an Athlete, 27

CHAPTER 7
Rich Experiences in the U.S. Army, 31

CHAPTER 8
Rich Experiences with Israel and the Jewish People, 39

CHAPTER 9
Rich Experiences with Japan and the Japanese People, 53

CHAPTER 10
Rich Experiences in Ukraine and with the Ukrainian People, 61

CHAPTER 11
Rich Experiences in Amateur Radio and Technology, 75

CHAPTER 12
Rich Experiences as an American, 79

CHAPTER 13
Conclusions on a Rich Life, 99

CHAPTER 1

Introduction

Background: The Great Depression

In 1929, the United States began its descent into the longest and most severe economic crisis in its history. The Depression began on October 29, 1929 with the collapse of the stock market, which immediately affected individuals whose assets were largely invested in stocks and those who had accumulated too much debt. In just two months, stockholders lost 40 billion dollars. By the end of 1930, the ripple effect of the collapse was felt by millions of US citizens. During the 1930s more than 9,000 banks failed. Unlike today, when bank deposits are insured, people lost their savings. Fear about the economy led people to stop buying consumer goods. The companies who made those goods were forced to lay off thousands, and the unemployment rate rose to 25 percent. Without jobs, many families could not make mortgage payments or pay other debt, so they lost their homes and possessions. One-half of all home mortgages were in default by the end of 1933. Franklin D. Roosevelt became the US President in that same year, and immediately instituted a series of economic programs called The New Deal. These programs created work for many of the unemployed, and began the long road back to a more stable economy. However, the nation did not truly recover from the Great Depression until the US military geared up for World War II, creating an urgent need for planes, ships and other items.

During the deep Depression of the 1930s my mother would gather her six children and put her arms around us and say, "Aren't we rich?" I was the oldest boy in the family and even though we didn't have anything to our name—no wealth at all—I didn't question at all the veracity of that statement. She would say it more than once on different occasions. Each time I personally felt that we were rich. We were not only rich in love for each other, but also rich in values of life which meant the most. We all played musical instruments and appreciated church music as well as the classics. We participated with others in orchestras, ensembles, and bands. We were very active in church activities and devoted to the Lord. My mother, a one-room-school teacher, passed on her high value for education to all of her six children, each of whom obtained a college degree.

When I listen to the news at night, I can say to myself, "I have been there, done that, or met that person in my life's experiences."

Luncheon Interview with Dr. Seuss

Recently in the news I saw that an unpublished manuscript of the late Dr. Seuss had now been discovered. It brought to mind my own meeting with Dr. Seuss during the 1980s. As head of the Council of Great City Schools, I happened to be in California. While there I had a personal luncheon interview with Dr. Seuss. As a leading educator of the time, he wished to interview me as well. He wanted to learn my philosophy of education. I was interested to know the man who had influenced so many young lives.

I found the man to be quite ordinary, both in appearance and

My parents, Albert and Myrtle McMurrin, married in 1928 in Olin, Iowa.

LEFT: My grandfather Nathaniel McMurrin was a child when Lincoln was President. He immigrated from a farm in Scotland with his family. MIDDLE: My grandmother, Mary McMurrin. RIGHT: My maternal grandparents, the Brickleys, were farmers. My grandmother's father was in the Pennsylvania brigade in the Civil War.

LEFT: *The Antioch church, where my parents met. My father was the student pastor, came by train from Moody Bible Institute in Chicago each weekend.*
RIGHT: *The one-room schoolhouse where my mother taught, and where she was working when she met my father.*

in manner. I found it natural to call him Mr. Geisel. Years later, I am interested to see what that talented man still had up his sleeve at the time of his passing.

Interview with Dr. Bennett

In 1985, I had an interview with the young, newly appointed Secretary of Education. President Reagan chose William Bennett over a representative of the pro-confederacy, Dixiecrat faction of the Democratic party to lead the nation's Education Department. The 42 year old Bennett was from a middle class background, and attended private religious schools. His experience was in teaching and the philosophy of education.

At the time I was President of the Council of Great City Schools, with a good deal of experience working with and effecting change in urban schools. During the luncheon interview I found the man bright and thoughtful. However, I sensed his unease in his new position to lead all the nation's schools in an era of desegregation. We were both on a fact-finding mission.

I'm 85 years old and, as I review my life, I think of all the rich experiences I have had. So I want to record them for posterity.

CHAPTER 2

Rich Experiences in Family Life

Births of Siblings

The firstborn was my sister Norma, and I came along thirteen months later. By the time I was one, I was larger than my sister. Mother always expected me to watch after my "little sister." When off to school, I was admonished to "watch out for Norma." One day a playground ball hit her full in the face. I felt I had not done my duty; I took her home. With five brothers, Norma was a spunky girl. Little Norma was not the one left in charge of the brothers when our parents attended church meetings; it was Lee left in charge.

Since I was the oldest boy, I remember the births of three of my brothers. Nathan's birth I do not recall, since he was but a year younger than I. Growing up, he was of small stature. Mother called me "big boy" and Nathan "little boy."

My brother Paul was born in Huntingsburg, Indiana and he had a red birthmark on his forehead. Since we were poverty stricken, there was a debate as to whether we should pay for the medical procedure to remove the birth defect. I believe I contributed to the decision the family made to remove the birthmark, for it was growing and would eventually cover his entire face. I do not know how we paid for it, but it was removed.

Two years later, my brother Dwight was born in Corydon, Indiana. He had dark brown eyes and was a delightful baby. He would sit in the middle of the table and entertain with his bright eyes and smile. Corydon, the original capital of the state, experienced the 1937 Ohio River flood. In 1937 the Johnstown flood had a huge impact, not only in Pennsylvania, but affecting all those downstream along the Ohio River and into Indiana and beyond. Residents all along the way, already hard hit by years of the Depression, were further devastated by the ravishing flood damage.

At that time our family was living in Corydon. Our two story house was along a creek, back a mile off the Ohio River. The water rose steadily until the family was forced to move upstairs. The water occupied the first floor. Thus, the family had no heat. There were no kitchen facilities and limited plumbing, but we were all together. There we stayed until the waters receded. Oatmeal seemed to be the mainstay diet. Sometime during the course of the week or so, the health department came to our house in a boat, arriving at the second story window, informing us of the diphtheria epidemic. The men took my father and me to be vaccinated. There was an epidemic, and the health authorities wanted to be certain heads of household were protected.

When the waters receded we came downstairs to face the huge cleanup task. A photo of us children on a stump soon after showed hollow eyes

My sister Norma was 3 and I was 2 when this portrait was taken.

This photo with my mother was taken after the 1937 Johnstown flood when I was about 6, Norma 7, Nate 5 and Paul, 3. We all were happy to have survived.

with bags beneath, skinny and bedraggled bodies. But, we were all safe, all together.

Dwight, in his early years had pneumonia twice, but he survived his delicate childhood health. Very bright, he taught himself to read and was allowed to attend school at five. He was taken to upper grades classrooms to demonstrate reading with expression.

Two years later my brother Roger was born in Bedford, Indiana. My mother was to have her first hospital birth, but Roger came before she arrived at the hospital. We were all farmed out with members of the church. I went to the Sunday school superintendent's home, along with my brother Paul. I remembered my mother nursed Roger, but she became so busy, having to move once again, she put him on formula. He developed colic, and mother had to resort to goat's milk to feed him. Roger was remembered as a crying baby. Mother was often up at night with him. A church member, seeing the light on at the parsonage past midnight, went to the church board to condemn the family as spendthrifts. The consequence was to cut the weekly salary from $15 to $12 a week to cover the additional parsonage electricity costs.

Gardening

Family tradition was having a garden, so during the Depression it was important to have a garden; then when WWII came along, we all had Victory Gardens. During certain seasons we had surplus. We would take our produce in the little red wagon down the street selling the fresh vegetables. Father had a statement that "Our Basket should be full and overflowing." Our neighbors looked forward to the overflow from that garden.

As a family we did a lot of canning of surplus vegetables, particularly tomato juice. At various parsonages, we also had fruit trees and so we had cherries and "apple jam." To make the preserves, we had a huge pot outside over an open fire. The fruit would cook, and we would stir for hours, until it was jam.

This bicycle was my Christmas gift when I was 9. The caveat was that it should be shared with my siblings.

Family Christmas

The family Christmases hold many fond memories. Even though we were poor, my parents wanted us to have good Christmases complete with presents. There were two family relatives who made Christmas special. My mother's only sister sent everyone socks every Christmas; we all looked forward to that. My father lost his father when he was fourteen years old, and he went to work for a distant cousin, who had a rich 640 acre farm in Iowa. At Christmastime, this relative sent a substantial check. The Strivers family made years of bright Christmases for the McMurrin family. As eldest boy, I usually received a special present. Early on, the present was a bright red wagon, a very special wagon with balloon tires and a chrome railing around the top, as well as a chrome bumper and sideboards. This beauty was to be shared with all the brothers. When I was nine years old, I received a bicycle for Christmas. To me, it was the best bicycle made, with whitewall tires, a front light, rear reflector and a basket. It, too, came with the caveat: it was to be shared. Share I did, though I grumbled when the brothers had a wreck or two with it.

My father was always a pastor of a church. Each year, on the Sunday evening before Christmas, there was a special music service, and giving of gifts. There were also some plays and cantatas. I remember all the supportive parents cueing their children in their parts from the audience.

My Family Supported the Wars

My father grew up during the First World War, but he was too young to be inducted into the service. My mother's older brother was part of the Expedition Force that went to France. My father was a little too old to be drafted in the Second World War, and he had a family of six children, but he did work in the support effort. He worked at a factory that made tanks, while my mother worked at a canning factory. There, the men bringing the produce to her wore large POW initials on the back of their shirts; these were German Prisoners of War. My mother said they were such fine young men.

During the Korean War, three of us brothers were of an age to be drafted. My brother Nathan went to Miami University in Ohio and registered for Air Force ROTC. He graduated with honors as a distinguished officer, and became a pilot for multi-engine bombers, like the B-17. He registered a complaint to his superiors that some of his crew came on board in the morning still under the influence of liquor. Since he needed an alert crew at each station on the B-17, he feared for their safety. He informed his superiors of his concerns, and they did nothing to address his complaint, so he wrote a letter to the Pentagon, expressing his concerns about the crew's drinking habits. They wrote him back, saying that drinking and flying went together. They stated his views were incompatible with Air Force policy, and he was issued an honorable discharge.

On the beach at Pensacola, Florida where my brother Paul was training to be a Navy pilot.

My brother Paul joined the Navy ROTC at Miami University. He graduated as a Navy officer, and went to Pensacola, Florida after graduation to train as a Navy pilot. He found out that his peripheral vision was not adequate to land a plane on an aircraft carrier, so he became the captain's assistant on the Forrestal and traveled to all the ports of the world where America had an interest.

Paul was allowed to go ashore with the captain's permission to explore each of the ports. I asked where the most beautiful women in the world resided. He replied Johannesburg, South Africa. There, pre-Apartheid, women of many ethnic cultures had married and produced beautiful combinations of features and skin shades, he said.

Being of draft age, each year at university I had to pass a rigorous test to be exempt from going into service. I went to Miami University in Ohio, along with about 500 other students, to take these tests; each year I was exempted. After graduation, I taught fifth grade at Sharonville, Ohio for one year. The following October I received my draft notice; it seemed the board had run out of draftees, so despite being a classroom teacher, I was off to the Korean War.

CHAPTER 3

Rich Work Experiences in My Youth

As the oldest boy in the family, there were always chores to do at home. At an early age I would be responsible for our home, since my mother and father were off to meetings they had to attend. Sometimes I would make popcorn for my younger brother and my older sister. The house had to be in good care when my parents returned and the children were heading off to bed for the night. Later on, as we move from place to place, I would do gardening by hand.

We lit the cooking range in the kitchen with available fuel. Sometimes, for a quick hot fire, we would use corn cobs that we got for free from the nearby grain elevator. We would pull carts we made behind our bicycle to haul the load of cobs back to the house.

In Bedford, Indiana during the deep Depression we raised rabbits for pets and, on occasion, had fresh rabbit meat. We fed the rabbits greens we would pick up at the grocery stores, which were thrown away as garbage.

In Mohawk, Indiana during the war the price of eggs went sky high, so I started a flock of chickens in the attic of the garage so I could make some money. The price of eggs dropped dramatically and we ended up eating a lot of chicken for Sunday dinner.

During WWII there were no young men around to do farm work. I would go with my father to help farmers harvest wheat, hay and corn crops. The farmers found that I was a good size and that I was a good worker, so they would have me drive tractors to plow the fields and disc the plowed land ready for planting. Also, I worked behind a horse planting tomatoes, using equipment that would deposit water and put a slit in the soil for the tomato plants. You had to be quick to deposit the tomato plant every time when it clicked. Also, during the summer months, I cultivated the fields of corn and soy beans with the tractor.

Working in a Canning Factory

At the age of fourteen I went to work for a canning factory that canned tomatoes in many different varieties and other vegetables, such as carrots, beets, and cabbage for sauerkraut.

Getting ready for the canning season, I would work with an engineer to design and repair the assembly lines and canning equipment. The owner thought I could do many tasks. One that was particularly challenging for me was making cement platforms to put the equipment off the floor so the legs wouldn't rust and fall apart. The owner was surprised that I hadn't learned to do this in school. "Don't they teach you anything worthwhile in school nowadays?" I learned many things here on the job.

The canning factory sold tomato plants to the farmers. I learned to design hot beds to start the growth of the plants in early spring. I also made wooden boxes to put them in for planting and harvesting to the farmer.

During the busy summer canning season I worked on the assembly line and kept a long table full of produce where many ladies would sort the produce, each ready for the next procedure.

I designed a conveyor that would save the jobs of two workers. The engineer put it all together and the owner called me into his office to give me a raise from 30 cents an hour to 35 cents an hour. He took me on as a confidant and told me that workers were stealing cans of vegetables from him each day. When asked what he intended to do about it, he replied, "Nothing." I assumed he believed that it would set a division between him and his workers, costing more to enforce than what the few stole.

His attitude was a rich learning experience that I could apply in later life as a teacher and school administrator. "Don't make a mountain out of a mole hill." Don't let small infractions take away from the major purpose and goal.

CHAPTER 4

Rich Experiences with Family —A Talented Wife as Homemaker

Frances Had a Limited Environment Growing Up
My wife was born in a one room cabin in southern Georgia. It was made of pine planks with a tin roof, and she could see the chickens under the house through the gaps in the floor. When her mother took the children and went to Florida to live with the grandparents on a truck farm south of Daytona Beach, she had many rich experiences during the WWII years. She saw war ships patrolling the coast along Daytona Beach looking for subs. At night, German submarine crews would come ashore on the beach. Grandfather's home had to have black shades on all the windows. At night they had a battery powered radio; all would gather quietly around it to hear the war news. Her grandfather built his own truck to take vegetables to market; it did not have a windshield. The garden was cultivated entirely with hand tools. It was a very primitive way of living, but grandfather was a self-made man.

Her mother worked as many as three jobs to support her girls. She eventually moved her two girls to a home she purchased in

Daytona Beach. She ran a restaurant, where the girls did chores. The girls had a chance to go to a nearby elementary school. Frances was disturbed to see colored workers going to work early in the morning step off the sidewalk to allow white pedestrians to pass.

Meeting Frances While in the Army at Ft. Benning, GA

The family moved to Columbus, Georgia where the girls attended Jordan High School. While Frances was in high school I dated her and saw her graduate. Her girlfriends asked her why she was dating this "old" soldier; I was twenty three at the time. I met Frances at a Youth for Christ meeting held in a civic hall. There were two organizations in the south that would not allow segregation. One was Youth for Christ; the other was Billy Graham's ministry. On base at Ft. Benning, black and white soldiers could worship together in the chapel; they could also be together at the Youth meeting. At this meeting, Frances sat in the front row. The soldiers sat in the second row, directly behind the girls. I knew one of the girls and we decided to drive our cars to the Steak and Shake Drive-in. Another soldier and I were invited to sit in the back seat of her car. Frances was in the front passenger seat. The driver admitted that Frances was shy. She did not talk much, nor did she turn around. The next day I called the driver and asked who the passenger was. "Is she pretty? She has a nice back of the head." She admitted she was pretty and agreed to give me the girl's telephone number. That's where it all began.

Dating Frances

Frances and I, not having much money, had many picnics. Two delicacies were pineapple and banana sandwiches. We also went swimming together at the public lakes. I went to her home numerous times, where I would play the trumpet and she the piano. She worked to purchase her own piano, and to take music lessons. Eventually I was discharged and returned to my home in Cincinnati, Ohio. Back in Daytona Beach, Frances went to work for Commercial Credit as a treasurer, and accounted for all the money and financial accounts. I would make occasional weekend visits to spend time with her. Our correspondence was intense; we wrote wonderful letters back and forth, some of which I still have.

Frances Visits Leetonia, Ohio

Frances came from Florida to visit me in Leetonia, Ohio. At that time I was a school administrator over four elementary schools. I went to Pittsburgh to pick her up from the central railroad depot. I met every train coming from Washington, DC. She was not on any of the trains. Finally, I asked if there was another train station in Pittsburgh. There was—the Chesapeake & Ohio Railroad station. I rushed to the second location, finding it nearly empty. There on a bench, in a beautiful hat, surrounded by luggage, was Frances, ready to go home, thinking she had been stood up.

Asking Frances to Marry Me

Later, we returned to Pittsburgh for a classical organ concert. Following the performance, in a nearby park, I asked Frances to marry me. She accepted; she went home—on an airplane—with a diamond ring. It was a direct flight; I didn't want her to go through the misery of another rail journey.

Getting Married and Returning to Leetonia

We got married that August at the First Baptist Church in Daytona Beach, and then returned to Leetonia in her Plymouth coupe, U-Haul trailer with all her possessions in tow. Having spent our last money on the Pennsylvania Turnpike, we arrived penniless and nearly without gas at a furnished home I had rented for

Frances – a beautiful lady who liked to dress up and made life so beautiful and comfortable for her family.

us. One concern she had was of living up to social expectations of a school administrator's wife in Leetonia. Leetonia had almost no social expectations; she did fine.

Frances Decorates

As a school administrator moving up the ladder, we had to make several important moves. We moved to Dover, Ohio where I became Elementary Supervisor. I was still working under the supervision of Dr. Paul C. Hayes, who was also moving up the ladder. We bought a relatively new home that needed a lot of decorating and furnishing. This is where my daughter Michelle was born. Frances decorated a nursery with animals and birds on the walls and a new crib with mobile objects. She even painted a dresser so it fit the decor of the room. She gave the same creative and delicate touches to the entire house. Though the yard was small, she decorated it as well with shrubs and flowers.

Frances Decorates Home in Grove City, Ohio

From there we moved to Grove City, Ohio and the Superintendent and I became the only central office administrators of the largest suburban school district in Ohio. Our offices were in an old farm house, which was somewhat dilapidated. I had an upstairs office with a secretary. The teachers we were recruiting had to come up the wooden steps. One day a tall and gangly woman came up the wooden steps in heels so clumsily I feared she might trip and go out the window, which was at the end of the stairway. Her appearance denoted that, though from the South, she was not a refined Southern lady. In the interview I found out she really loved children, and was capable. Feeling she would make a good teacher, I called a school principal whose building was on the same site as the central offices. I told her not to rely on her first impressions. She later called and told me she wanted to keep the teacher.

She felt she would be good for the children. On visiting her school, I saw her on the playground towering like a giant above the little children, and they simply adored her. It was evident from the way they gathered around her.

Dr. Paul Hayes Becomes the Superintendent of Schools of Southwestern City Schools

Doctor Hayes was a mentor of mine for many years. I followed him in his moves up the administration ladder, this time to the headquarters of the district in Grove City, Ohio. Here we acquired a basically new home that needed everything done to it: screens, storm windows, carpets and window treatments, as well as the task of developing the yard. Frances took on the task of developing the house. We both took on the yard. We put in a cement driveway, and I lined it with petunias. Here was the town where Michelle entered kindergarten. First day we both had tears, but she was very happy to be the first one to go off to school.

Frances decorated a new nursery and both Marianne and Marshall were born in Grove City at a Columbus hospital. The morning following my son's birth, at the principals' meeting I announced that my son "Marshall Lee" had been born. A principal asked, "Why didn't you call him 'General Lee'?"

We remained in Grove City for several school years, during which time there was tremendous growth. Year after year we had to pass levies and build new schools. One year we built three elementary schools and three middle schools.

We Move to Toledo, Ohio

In 1965 I was recruited by the new superintendent of the Toledo public schools. After several interviews he hired me as his assistant, and now the family had to move to a new location once more. This time I bought a beautiful brick home in a part of Toledo

We bought this home in Milwaukee from the Case family, as a result of Frances complimenting Mrs. Case on the design of the home.

Frances decorated our homes, including one in Milwaukee, Wisconsin. In this bedroom she used sheets to cover the walls like wallpaper. She also created the headboard and sewed the cover on the bench.

filled with outstanding architectural brick and stone homes in the vicinity of the University of Toledo. Now my wife had an older home to remodel and decorate, a basement and three full stories. She designed a new kitchen with all the latest appliances and a new flooring of sturdy carpet. In this house there were bedrooms for each of the children. She individualized each room with coordinated decor from the bedding and walls to the cornices. She did all the window dressings for the entire house. She also developed the music room by closing off a sunny sitting room adjacent to the living room. Plaques of children playing instruments decorated the walls. Frances' childhood upright had a place of honor, and the girls took piano lessons. I had my trumpet. Marshall's interest ran toward drums.

Move to Milwaukee Home

In 1975 I became the new superintendent of schools in Milwaukee, Wisconsin. Again, we searched for a comfortable home. I was a busy new school superintendent but my wife explored some of the finest homes in the city. She really enjoyed visiting Mrs. Case in a large stone home. Even the garage was stone with a slate roof. Mrs. Case was a former public school teacher; her deceased husband was a member of the Case family that owned the heavy equipment firm. Mrs. Case had to sell the home, for it had become too much for her to take care of. The house was in a trust at the First Wisconsin Bank. The trust officer wanted $120,000 for the house. Mrs. Case told Frances she was the only one who had complimented on the design of her classic home; in addition she was aware that her husband was the new superintendent. We scraped all our money together and put in a bid of $87,500. Mrs. Case told the trust officer to accept the bid of the new superintendent and his wife.

Frances Decorates New Home

Frances took on the challenge of the classic beauty. She designed a kitchen with the latest appliances, off of which she carved a breakfast nook from a storage room. Again, she used her creative and artistic talents to transform each room of the house. Again, she decorated each of the four bedrooms. The old floral wallpaper was removed and replaced with printed bed sheets; she had seen the technique in a Ladies Home Journal. She added all the matching pieces to decorate the room, being an able upholsterer and seamstress. She decorated the windows, the lamp stands, the footstools. All coordinated to make a grand effect in each room.

CHAPTER 5

Rich Experiences in Music

Sang on the Radio

My father was an associate pastor of a church in Evansville, Indiana. He was assigned to give an early morning devotion on the radio, since he had a very rich radio voice. At one of these morning devotions my brother Nathan, who was three, I, who was four, and my sister, who was five years old, sang a hymn. My brother believed the music was in three parts on one of these programs. My father was very interested in having us participate in church activities at a very young age. I recall the three of us singing at a special Sunday morning worship.

Took Lessons on Piano

Our family was very musical. Each one in the family had his own special talent and interest. My mother made sure that, even during the Depression, we took piano lessons. I took my first lesson at the age of seven. I still remember numbers that I played at the teacher's recitals. As I became older, the piano teacher told my mother that I had reached my plateau and that I should follow other interests in music.

Singing at Intermission at High School Plays

Our family members often performed music at intermission at high school senior plays. One year, as a first grader, my brother Paul sang God Bless America during the intermission. As a trio, my older sister, brother, and I sang in parts at these intermissions.

Free Music Lessons at Indiana Schools

Even though some of the schools were very small, they made sure they had a concert orchestra and a marching band that could go to statewide music contests. I took my first trumpet lessons in the fifth grade and soon joined the school's band. Each member of our family took lessons on his or her selected instrument. As I furthered my education I had the experience of playing the trumpet in the first chair in high school and college bands.

My Family Enjoyed Classical Music

Our home was filled with music; most of it was classical. As an educator, teachers asked me, "How do you get children to enjoy classical music?" My response was to give them the opportunity to hear classical music.

Church Hymns Ring in my Ears

Since we grew up with church music I can leaf through a hymnal and realize that I know most of the hymns. Often I wake up in the morning with a hymn ringing in my ears, which may stay with me most of the day.

CHAPTER 6

Rich Experiences as an Athlete

Learning Indiana Basketball

My first fourteen years of life were in Indiana. Since my father was a minister, we moved around a lot. He established many churches as well as served many small villages and country churches in Indiana. Therefore, I attended many different schools and had an Indianan tradition of playing basketball at an early age. In grade school the coach would throw out maybe ten basketballs in the old gym. It was like a free for all, where you would run, rebound, and shoot. In second grade we had an organized team which played at half time during a varsity basketball game on Friday nights. Moving up the grades I learned to play what Ohio called Indiana basketball.

The Championships in High School (Ohio)

When I was fourteen we moved to Walbridge, Ohio where my freshman basketball coach said he was going to rid me of the

Indiana basketball's ridiculous shots, such as the jump shot. He taught me how to shoot standing flatfooted, rolling the basketball and pushing it up toward the goal.

As a freshman, I was on the first five of the reserve team, so I would stay dressed and sit on the bench at the varsity game. One night we were getting beaten badly, so the coach put me in to the game. Since I was put into tight spots I spontaneously reverted back to Indiana basketball. He called timeout, called me to the side of the court and told me that from now on I could use Indiana basketball to help win games.

We had a very small high school with only 36 boys enrolled from 9th thru 12th grades. All but two brothers played basketball. As a senior I was the point guard and captain of the team. We had a very successful season with very tall basketball players. The Wood County tournament was held at the Bowling Green State University gym, which was the largest gym that we had ever seen. We won five games to become county champions. Some of the gyms we played at during the school year were so small that the center circle intersected with the other two circles on the floor and the basketball backboard was against the wall. One gym had a pot belly stove at the center circle, which heated the entire gym. Another gym had such a low ceiling that the lights were covered with protective steel baskets, and if you had a long shot, you would have to negotiate the shot between the baskets that were on the low ceiling.

Athletics in College

In 1948 I enrolled at Olivet Nazarene College. This was the time that GIs were returning from World War II. Facilities were crowded and our bunk beds were assembled in an abandoned bowling alley. The windows were so porous that, during winter snow storms, snow would collect at the foot of our beds.

Once girls began moving into their new dorm, the top floor of the girl's old dorm became available for male students. We were to play an exhibition game in the Kankakee basketball arena. We were scheduled to play the city's industrial team. The local newspaper featured a story before the scheduled game. They said the Olivet Nazarene College players were a bunch of sissies, since they lived in the girls' old dorm. I was determined to prove we were not sissies and we would beat the industrial league team. I must admit I did hog the ball that night and scored 43 points.

The football coach saw me play basketball in my freshman year and that summer he invited me out for a football practice. He said I was tall and had good hands and I could jump, and that I would make a good receiver. At the first practice I went out for a long pass and caught it, then froze in my tracks. He yelled at me and said I was supposed to run to the goal. I told him I had never seen a football game; at that time there was no TV to show a game being played. Since the high school was very small there were not enough boys to suit up a team. Even so, he told me that I had better stick to basketball.

At a springtime track and field meet I was not on the team, but was participating by selling Coke out of a galvanized tub filled with crushed ice. The track coach approached me saying he didn't have anyone entering the standing high jump event. I told him that I had never seen anyone do that event before and I would not be a good contender. He said he had seen me jump in basketball games and I would make at least a respectable showing. He showed me how to jump over the bar, so I followed his instructions. I won a blue ribbon by jumping 4 feet 6 inches. Before the next year's track and field meet I practiced so I would be ready for the standing high jump event. This is an event where you stand at the bar and spring over it. In my case they kept raising the bar and I would clear it every time. I had no trouble going up over the bar. It was the landing on wood chips that hurt. They raised the bar to 5 feet and they said that I cleared it by two inches. They tried to persuade me to jump again. They said that I had now set a new college record. At this moment my right arm was bleeding and I felt that I had jumped enough. Someone in the crowd said that for a school record you had to measure the lowest spot on the bar and the highest spot on the ground. Since I had made several tries to clear the bar the ground was packed down where I stood to set the record. However, they measured directly under the bar which was much higher. I also had to clear the highest part of the bar not the lowest. Anyway, the record was set at a fraction below 5 feet and that is the record that has not been broken. They don't hold that event anymore.

Many years later I returned to Olivet Nazarene University to receive the Athletic Hall of Fame Award for the record I achieved: playing four years of basketball, and one event in track and field. I thought to myself that they should have athletes try to break this standing high jump record by putting up the standards and positioning the bar at 5 feet to see if someone could clear it. I refrained myself from this offer. Now the record will stand forever.

CHAPTER 7

Rich Experiences in the U.S. Army

Introduction to the Army

In 1953 I was drafted out of the classroom as a teacher into the Korean War. I said goodbye to family and school friends and was inducted in Cincinnati, Ohio. I went to Fort Knox, Kentucky for the first night away from home. Fort Knox is the place that our gold reserves are stored, but for the draftees, it was a place to get your Army uniform, boots, and a duffle bag full of extras. From Fort Knox we flew into Camp Rucker, Alabama for eight weeks of basic training.

On approaching Fort Rucker from the air, it looked like we were going to a prison camp. There were no trees or grass and there was a checkered water tank that held the only color present at the camp. The cadre in charge of our basic training was from the South. Our first experience at Camp Rucker was being ordered with our duffle bags and everything we owned to the barracks. They would say we went to the wrong barracks and say we were a

I received my Army training at Camp Rucker, Alabama. Here I am seen in full uniform at attention.

bunch of "Northern fools." Then they would order us to a barracks on the second floor. Once there, they would tell us how foolish we were because they just wanted us to go to the first floor. This, then, was our introduction into the Army: learning to take orders and feeling like a fool.

Experience with My Rifle

On the rifle range I learned the Army's way of firing an M-1 rifle. I had never fired a weapon before but I took the instructions very seriously. I must have had a high score at the rifle range because I was recommended for the base rifle team. I was assigned to make my first appearance on Saturday after being on guard duty all night, so I didn't have a chance to shave. I went to the supply Sergeant and asked for my rifle, which I kept clean and well lubricated. For some reason, he wouldn't give it to me. I protested to him that I was going to the rifle range for the base general had invited me to be on the base rifle team. He made me take the rifle he held out. "In this man's army, one rifle is as good as another." I didn't argue with him, but I knew it wasn't true. Some soldiers in the barracks polished their rifle inside and out so they would receive compliments on inspection, but steel wool will take off the sharpness of the rifling.

At the rifle range, I adjusted the rifle and began firing at the target. I didn't hit the bull's eye; I didn't even hit the large target. The General came up to me and asked what the problem was. I replied I didn't have my rifle because the supply Sergeant wouldn't give it to me and he instead gave me this "piece of junk." The General said to me, "In this man's army one rifle is as good as another." Since he was a general and I was a private I did not try to correct him. He told me I didn't know how to adjust the rifle and that I needed a shave, so I was dismissed from the base rifle team.

Moving to Fort Benning, Georgia

The Third Infantry Division moved from Camp Rucker to Fort Benning, Georgia on a long march. I didn't make this trip because I was already assigned to radio school at Fort Benning. With my background in education I recognized that this was one of the finest schools of which one could ever be a part. In public schools, such as in science classes, there is one microscope for all students to take turns looking at the specimen on the slide. At this school, every student's station had all the equipment necessary to do the testing and basic operations. We had instructors, often two, that complemented each other, and tests were taken at the end of each day to see if we had learned all that was being taught. The evaluators assessed the instruction and the next day there would be new mockups illustrating the radio theory. The parts that were missed by the students would be re-taught. I personally had a lot of background in radio because I built them as an elementary school student when my family listened to short wave from Russia, Great Britain, and Cuba during WWII. I wanted to be a ham radio operator with license to broadcast, but no such licenses were given during WWII. I now have a letter on file from the commanding general commending me for making the highest scores ever on the daily and final tests that were given.

Part of the First Integrated Army

The Army was segregated with black and white units, but President Truman gave an executive order to integrate all military units. Thus, at Fort Benning, we had both black and white soldiers training together in the Third Infantry Division. It was anticipated there would be many problems with the integrated Army, but as far as I experienced, there were none. However, when we went together into Columbus, Georgia it was still very segregated. The bus stops had separate restrooms and water fountains, one for colored ONLY, and another for whites. However, at one bus stop the city installed one refrigerated fountain, which was a significant upgrade, but they couldn't afford two. Therefore, one side of the fountain was white only and the other was for colored only, but it was the same water. Black soldiers got a laugh at this absurdity. Also, on base we worshiped together at the chapel, sometimes with black speakers and sometimes with white, and there was never a problem. However, in the town or Columbus, Georgia it was still segregated so colored soldiers weren't allowed into the Protestant churches. There were two organizations that required integrated services. Billy Graham's team required no separation; Youth for Christ required no separation of colored and whites, either. Each had both white and black speakers.

Army Maneuvers at Fort Hood, Texas

The Third Infantry Division went by trucks and jeeps to Fort Hood, Texas to face the First Armored Division in maneuvers. On the way to Texas, we ran into rainstorms so we put the covers on the trucks and ponchos on ourselves to stay dry. The Colonel told us to take it off because he didn't want to see a ragged army going through a small town in the South, so we went through towns wet.

Facing the First Armored Division at Fort Hood, we had to be alert day and night. We had to dig in and make deep fox holes, anticipating being run over by tanks. We did set up a perimeter to protect ourselves, but at night we could hear the tanks rolling. In the morning we came upon the Colonel stalled on the road. When we approached his jeep, we learned his radio operator had told him he could fix the radio. Since I was the radio man of our battalion, the Colonel wanted to know if I could fix the radio. I told him I could smell a short in the radio. He had to get a new radio; this one couldn't be fixed in the field. He liked that I knew about radios and wanted me to be his radio operator, so I joined him. As radio operator, I sat in the back of the jeep. Even so, I detected the colonel was unable to clearly read a map. When the General came

I was a private first class in the 3rd Infantry Division in the Army at age 23.

up to check on things, he would pull it to himself as if he could read; the driver was the only one who could read a map, but the Colonel was a take-charge kind of guy.

The Colonel led the convoy up into the mountains, which was a dead end. He pranced around and fussed about it and didn't know what to do. I thought to myself, "We were going to war with these people and they are getting us stuck at a dead end?" Luckily, there was a skilled Sergeant who proposed making a circle and breaking down the bushes so we could turn around and escape. At night the Colonel would have us dig fox holes so we would not get run over by tanks. The draftees in this unit were all highly educated so we would read softback books while waiting for orders. He would come tell us we were a bunch of "educated fools" and we had to bury our books.

Attended Southern Baptist Churches

The Southern Baptist Churches welcomed soldiers to worship with them and I found they had many ministries, even some special ones for soldiers. Once one of the pastors called a group of soldiers into his office after service and dictated letters to each of our parents saying we had attended service.

Rose through the Ranks in the Army

My final assignment in the Army at Fort Benning was to head up the radio maintenance shop. Since I was in charge, they wanted to give me a rank of Specialist, so I received the specialist patches to put on my uniform. Now I was in charge of keeping all radios and phones in good order as well as teaching the novices about radio maintenance. I was discharged after eighteen months, since the Korean War was over and they wanted to reduce the number of soldiers.

CHAPTER 8

Rich Experiences with Israel and the Jewish People

In my 85 years of life, I remember numerous face to face and actual experiences with the nation of Israel and with the Jewish people. I'm now going to list some of those.

Jewish Doctors Provide Free Service to Minister's Family
In my childhood my father, who was a minister of the gospel, would take us to the doctor. Often, these would be Jewish physicians, who would never charge him for their service. There were six of us children, so there were plenty of reasons to go to the doctor. This took place many times during my early years.

Serving as Superintendent of a Jewish School District
As a school superintendent I served seven years in the Beachwood City Schools (Ohio), which was 90 percent Jewish population. At

TOP: Shaker Heights home, before we had the exterior paint removed.
BOTTOM: Same home after we had the exterior restored to its original glory.

one time I had five Jewish lawyers on the Board of Education. They were very conscious of the fact that I made the Beachwood schools absolutely excellent. The city's schools became known as the finest schools in the state of Ohio. As result of this, I was invited to testify before a federal judge in Lawrence County who was determining the quality of education in Ohio. I was there before the court several days. At the end of my testimony the judge said that he wanted the children in his family to have the same quality education as we had in Beachwood Ohio. He wished they could go to our schools.

We had a number of synagogues in the area, some within the school district, and some just outside. I was often invited to speak to their congregations on issues relating to education.

While in Beachwood, I made arrangements with the nearest synagogues that their preschoolers and staff could come to our kindergarten school if they came under threat, and that our children could go to their facilities if we came under threat. It should be known that one Saturday the Nazis completely destroyed one of our kindergarten classrooms and left their swastikas on our building, so these threats weren't to be thought of as only verbal; they were actual occurrences.

Rich Experiences as Superintendent of Schools in Milwaukee, Wisconsin

While superintending schools in Milwaukee, Wisconsin, I was asked by a Rabbi from one of the most influential synagogues in the area to speak at the Friday night service. We were constantly in the news because we were integrating the schools under a federal court order. Some of the school districts in suburban areas that had large Jewish populations were invited to exchange students with us, so this subject was of great interest to the Jewish population. The wife and I had dinner with the Rabbi and his wife before the service and I thought I'd use a quote from Isaiah, "Justice shall roll down like a mighty stream." He said that quotation was not from Isaiah, it was in Amos. I am glad he corrected me. The audience was very attentive to my presentation; afterward everyone was invited to the recreation room to voice their concerns and present questions to me.

I had one more invitation to the synagogue on a week night. I was invited to make a presentation on why I, as a Christian, go to church regularly. There was a study out of Chicago (in which Milwaukee was included) centered on the subject of why synagogues were losing attendance at services and how they could gain it back. They thought my ideas on including youth in the services were helpful.

The First Visit to Israel

While an officer in the Council of the Great City Schools, I was invited, along with the superintendent of Atlanta, Georgia schools to go to Israel. We were to negotiate a contract to exchange students with the largest cities in America. On that trip I had wonderful contacts with the heads of government in Israel and learned they exchanged 2,000 students with West Germany every year. The students were to spend time with their exchange families learning about the Jewish culture and schools. My wife went with me on this trip, and the Milwaukee Jewish Community Center paid for all of her expenses.

Visit to Holocaust Museum in Jerusalem

In front of the Holocaust Museum is a sculpture of the Warsaw warriors who resisted the Nazis. Several dark figures commemorated the resistance. Inside the museum were the Nazis' records of goals and results from the internment camps. The immaculate records noted gold teeth extracted, jewelry and shoes taken, deaths per day; all was recorded. There also were letters written to President Roosevelt and Prime Minister Churchill by Jewish lead-

Lee R. McMurrin | 43

TOP: *Jewish children doing exercises at school.* MIDDLE: *Children lining up at a school in Israel.* BOTTOM: *Jewish school students armed with weapons in Israel.*

ers, urging the bombing of the camps. My wife, who accompanied me, saw and heard of some of these atrocities for the first time, since she was younger than I. When we came out of the museum, she sat down on the curb and wept for nearly thirty minutes. Also moving was a garden outside the museum dedicated to the 'Righteous Gentiles' who put their own lives at risk to aid Jewish people.

Wife Hosting Bible Study

Because of her many experiences with Jewish people, she had an abiding loyalty for them through the years. While I was a busy superintendent in Milwaukee, my wife hosted two Jewish groups in our home for Bible study.

Attended Friday Night Services with Jewish Families

In the Toledo neighborhood in which we lived there were many Jewish families. Some were members of the school system. On occasion, our families went to the traditional Friday night services at the synagogue together. This was a part of my children's upbringing to further acquaint them with Jewish traditions that are part of our family values.

My Daughter Swims at the Jewish Community Center

During a teachers' strike in Milwaukee, my daughter damaged her hand severely while trying to go over a barbed wire fence surrounding the school's track field so the track team could practice. After that, she could no longer play basketball so she took up swimming. She practiced daily, without cost, at the Olympic size pool at the Jewish Community Center. Her high school swimming team became state champions in girls' swimming. My daughter was on the relay team, but they would win every event because they had an all American swimmer on their team.

TOP: *Sculpture of the Downtrodden at the Holocaust Museum in Tel Aviv.* MIDDLE: *The Wailing Wall, located in the old quarter of East Jerusalem in Israel, is a sacred place for Jews. Statue of Warsaw Warriors at the entrance to the Holocaust Museum, Tel Aviv, Israel.* BOTTOM: *Jewish soldiers guarding the gate to the Dome of the Rock in Jerusalem, a Muslim shrine built on the Temple Mount in AD 861.*

Superintendent of Tel Aviv, Israel Visits Milwaukee

The Tel Aviv superintendent of schools stayed in my home for several nights while visiting our specialty schools, known around the world as magnet schools. At dinner table discussions he related that, as a child, his education included memorization of books of the Bible as a disciplinary measure; thus, he assured us, he could quote several books of the Bible.

He was especially happy to visit the Golda Meir School for Gifted Children. This was on 4th street and the very school Golda attended at the turn of the century. As prime minister, she came to visit the 4th street School and the headline in the paper was "Mrs. Shalom revisits childhood school." In Israel you did not name a thing or a place after someone until they had died. Even though the school on 4th street was in a depressed area, the school was nicely integrated and became very popular.

Honored in Second Visit to Israel

My second invitation to visit Israel came from the new Minister of Education, who issued an invitation to join leading educators at a banquet to recognize and honor educators in Israel's schools. Of course I wasn't the only one honored, but he announced I was there because I had given him the inspiration to install thirteen magnet schools throughout Israel fashioned after the Milwaukee model. He also invited me to the Knesset, where they passed the law that would provide computers with access to the internet for all school aged children throughout Israel.

Visit to Golda Meir Nursery School

On my second visit to Israel, the Minister of Education offered a reciprocal treat; having visited the Golda Meir School for the Gifted in Milwaukee, he invited me to attend a Golda Meir nursery school, which was a real treat. They performed traditional dance and songs for me.

Golda Meir Nursery School, which I visited on my second trip to Israel.

The Deputy Mayor of Jerusalem Promoted School Integration

The Deputy Mayor of Jerusalem was very tall, stately and had a great presence; however, she stated without equivocation that she would never be reelected to office. She believed that Jerusalem's schools should be integrated, with both Jewish and Arab children attending classes together, and made certain this practice was put into in all new schools created.

Leadership Training for the Future

Within the city was a boarding school to train the nations' future leaders; this school had both Jewish and Arab students learning and living together in a successfully integrated program. Interestingly, a plaque stated that it was American funds that paid for the boarding facility.

Abraham Lincoln in Israel

In my tour of Israel they took me by the statue of young Abraham Lincoln. Alongside the full statue are quotes from the Gettysburg Address.

Leonard Tolstoy, the famous author of War and Peace, made a tour of cities, giving lectures on great men in Russian history. When he finished, they would say, "Now tell us about Abraham Lincoln."

Assassination of Israel's Prime Minister

I was getting ready to leave Tel Aviv to go home, standing in a long line in the airport, when a small radio announced the Prime Minister of Israel, Yitzhak Rabin, had been shot at a convention center just down the road from the airport. The police had already taken the assassin into custody. It was amazing that the routines at the airport went along as usual, no delays, and no cancellations. When I got to New York, all the newspapers had headlines about the Prime Minister being assassinated.

Honoring the Dead

I attended many Jewish funerals, in Milwaukee as well as Beachwood, Ohio. These services were very formal and traditional. Throughout the service, all men wore black dress hats. All family members were sequestered in an unseen area, and each service included a recitation of the 23rd Psalm. At these services, everyone was invited to the burial spot, and cars were provided for this. In Milwaukee I spoke at several of these memorials, since many were our very experienced staff members.

Devastating Effects of Polio

During the Polio epidemic in 1944, my four brothers, one at a time, contracted the disease. Thus, one of my brothers was severely affected with curvature of his spine growing up. When he was in his teens, a Jewish doctor from France came to Indianapolis Children's Hospital to perform a specialized operation, laying lamb bone all the way down his spine. This treatment for my brother came at no cost to our family. The doctor gave his time and the March of Dimes paid for all other expenses.

Involvement in the National Association for the Advancement of Colored People (NAACP)

Early in my career I became a lifetime member of NAACP. In the early history of this association, Jewish leaders helped sponsor and organize the organization. I was well acquainted with the Jewish superintendent of Rochester, New York. Doctor Goldberg told me that, at the Olympics in 1937 when he and Jesse Owens would tour Berlin, they found that most of the stores had signs stating No Jews or Negroes Allowed. Over the years the superintendent and Jesse Owens became the best of friends, of course, both suffering from this type of persecution. Dr. Goldberg became Deputy Secretary of Education, and was very helpful to me when we were integrating the city's schools in Milwaukee.

Jewish Experience in Ukraine

The purpose of the first visit to Ukraine was to see what my brother was doing as a music missionary. He had to have a Russian administrator, for he spoke no Russian, but had been able to gather up musicians to create the Kiev Symphony Orchestra and Chorus. Each musician belonged to the government; he had to obtain individual permission for each of the 165 musicians to perform. My brother became its conductor. Once again, Ukrainians enjoyed music not played for seventy years. He taught them to sing Handel's The Messiah in English.

A birthday party for the son (second from left) of the administrator of the symphony orchestra in Ukraine. The administrator's father (second from right) was a survivor of the Babi Yar massacre when he was 12 years old.

His chief administrator related an interesting story. When he got married, he took his wife's last name; being of part Jewish heritage, he was not allowed to become a citizen of Russia or of Ukraine, and had to carry identification showing he was a Jew.

Statue commemorating execution of 100,000 Jews murdered by the Nazis.

There's more to his family story than that. His father was twelve years old when the Germans invaded Ukraine. At first they thought of the Germans as liberators, for the Soviets took over and made it part of the Soviet Union. However, they soon learned that the Nazis were just as cruel. They invited all Jewish people to large city parks to receive instructions. Once assembled, the Germans opened up several Army trucks with mounted machine guns and opened fire, killing 100,000 Jews in one event. This massacre is known as Babi Yar. The twelve year old boy caught on early what was happening; he ran and ran far into a rural area, where he was raised by a Christian family.

I was invited to his son's home to visit. We visited the memorial commemorating the slaughter, a large mound of rusting steel, which is the ugliest monument I'd ever seen. The night of the visit it got so cold, but the family gave us their parkas so we could return to our apartment.

Four Bypass Surgery at Mount Sinai Hospital

I woke up one Sunday morning in 1996 and began to take my usual walk around the block. On the way I became very fatigued; I turned around and returned home. With my wife away caring for her mother, I called my daughter and told her that I was not feeling up to attending church. I then called my doctor, who was from the Ukraine, and left him a message on how I felt. He called back, and said that I should see him first thing Monday morning. By evening I felt nauseated and I leaned over the sink, though never vomited. I went to bed early. Next morning, I dressed and went to visit the doctor. In a few minutes I told him the story; he left the room. I later learned he was making arrangements for me to go to Mt. Sinai Hospital. Returning to the exam room, he gave me a large aspirin, and directed me to take a change of clothes and go to Mt. Sinai.

The receptionist at the hospital thought I was a salesman; I had to inform her I was there as a patient. They immediately began putting me through tests. I saw my closed arteries on the screen. A team of Jewish doctors scheduled me for surgery, which lasted four hours. They actually took my heart out of my chest, put it in a cooling box, and it quit beating. They told me I had a very healthy heart. When they reconnected everything, it started to beat on its own. When I awoke in intensive care, I wanted them to take out all the tubes in my mouth and nose; that is the only discomfort I felt. All the nurses left the room to attend to a heart patient they were losing. My wife was in Florida taking care of her dying mother. She was called to come be with me in recovery. She was so distressed, the staff actually put her in another room to be examined.

After a week or more in the hospital, I was ready to go home. I found my nurses on the benches outside smoking; I felt this was ironic since publicly posted in every room in the unit is a sign saying that smoking affects your heart. Once home, a nurse came daily to the home to check on me. My recovery was deemed complete.

Years later, at an airport checkpoint, the agent with the wand said, "What in the world do you have in your chest?" It was that I now had four staples in addition to the titanium in my left shoulder and hip.

Broken Wrist Operation at Mt. Sinai

Winter was coming, so that Saturday morning I intended to put a shield over the second story air conditioning unit. When I pushed the box onto the unit, the ladder slipped on the icy pavement. I fell two stories. I drove myself to the nearby St. Luke's Methodist Hospital. The doctors told me the wrist was broken in seven places. They said they could cast it, but the wrist would always be stiff. I did not like that prognosis, so I immediately called my primary doctor, a Jewish physician, who told me to get in my car, and head for Mt. Sinai Hospital. Dr. Wm. Seitz, known as the finest wrist and hand specialist in the world, examined me. Soon I was on the operating table. He braced my arm, and put in seven pins to hold the wrist bones together. After the operation, I stayed in the hospital for one day, and then was allowed to return home. The operation was very successful. The wrist healed completely, and after therapy was fully functional.

CHAPTER 9

Rich Experiences with Japan and the Japanese People

Japanese English Teachers Visit Milwaukee Schools
The group of about forty five teachers came to Milwaukee once a year to brush up on their English skills. They needed to work on pronunciation so that their English was understandable to Americans. During their ten day stay, they stayed with staff from the local schools and so learned about some of America's cultural traditions. In America there was a discussion about the young children learning songs which put African Americans in a negative light. The director of the Japanese teachers sat down at the piano and said, "This is a song every Japanese child learns," and she began playing "Old Black Joe." Surprisingly, there was a not a word, even an expression of reaction, from my staff.

Invitation from the Japanese Minister of Education
After a decade of visits, the Minister of Education invited me to come to Japan to evaluate the Japanese schools. From beginning to end, everything along the way was first class. Every attention was

taken to ensure my comfort. I took a Boeing 747 nonstop from Chicago to Tokyo. I was assigned the one seat in the front of the first class section, which was serviced by two airline hostesses. That journey provided a wealth of experiences.

Evaluation Report to Appear in Educational Journals

At the end of my visit I was invited to a multi-storied building that published educational journals. I was quizzed by several journalists on my impressions of Japanese schools. They were also interested in comparisons of those schools and ones in America. One main topic they wanted to discuss was the issue of bullying. This was a priority issue among educators and politicians in this nation. Each week in the national news there was a story about a child being bullied by others; some had committed suicide. At this time, bullying was not yet an issue in American schools. I told the journalists I was generally impressed with the decorum between teachers and students in their schools. I had expected a militaristic approach to education; I saw none of this. The teachers told me that brand of teacher was now gone; teachers mingle with the students, providing a pleasant atmosphere in the classroom.

Science and Math Classes in Elementary Schools

In America there would be just one microscope with a specimen. Children would line up to take a look; most saw their eyelashes. In the Japanese schools, each child had a microscope to do his own examinations. For the study of electricity, each child had his own circuit board, along with all the parts and wires, a power source and a switch to assemble a working buzzer. At first, each student worked on his or her own, but then they gathered into groups of five or six to share their experience. This was basically for troubleshooting, for not all the buzzers worked. They learned through their mistakes. The group that had the most experience with trouble shooting was featured; they were called upon to explain all their solutions.

In my tour of the school, I visited a math class. They had just finished an assignment. The teacher used mistakes that children had made as a learning tool. In some respects, those children were celebrated for they were making a significant contribution to the learning process. At least one would be called upon to put his problem solution on the chalkboard. This would be analyzed by the entire class, as to whether he had made any errors in calculations or process.

In American classrooms often the teacher highlights the students who make the correct calculations and do not correct the mistakes at that time. They move on to a new subject, without making sure each child understands what is taught. In doing so, they leave about one-third of the class behind.

Hiroshima Museum

At my visit to the museum, children were laying artificial flowers that they had created onto the monuments commemorating the dead at the nuclear bomb attack on the city. After laying their flowers in place, they would smile and engage me in English, anxious to try out their English phrases. There was no feeling of resentment or connection to the horrors of the war on their city. I went inside the museum where junior high students were putting notes in their tablets, taking in all the exhibits and relics and results from the atomic bomb. One of the relics was a city light post, which looked like an ice cream cone melting in the heat of the summer. It was now about three feet tall, and the glass dome had melted, running down over the bronze post. Another relic was a cement slab from a bridge, which had the shadows of people walking over the bridge. The people evaporated, leaving but a shadow on the concrete. Pictures showed water strewn with bodies of victims. I felt as MacArthur did that "Now I have seen the horrors of war..."

My First Host and Guide in Tokyo

A very short gentleman met me at the railroad station in Tokyo. He showed me my schedule, and presented me with an envelope with a hundred thousand yen and tickets for the bullet train. It seemed strange to me that he picked up my luggage. I was embarrassed that a man much smaller than I was going to carry my luggage. He did have fascinating stories. He related that in 1945 he was at the naval academy and about to be assigned to a battleship when the bomb exploded. He saw the flash in the sky and wondered what it was. Several days later he was told the war was over and he said he was very happy because he knew he would not survive on a Japanese battleship, since allied forces were sinking them right and left. Cadets were told to take off their uniforms and go home; the war was over. On hearing the news, he started walking home toward Tokyo. When he went through Hiroshima he saw the devastation. He continued walking towards Tokyo. He found Tokyo looked much as Hiroshima; it had been so extensively firebombed. He walked toward his neighborhood, and was pleased to see his police officer father walking his beat through the burned out streets, just as he had before the war.

Overnight Stay in the Deputy Minister of Education's Home

It was a wonderful privilege to spend a night in a family home. The host was a Harvard University graduate, and his wife accompanied him to America with the promise that he would provide her with an American kitchen on their return to Japan. They had three school aged children, and in this modern kitchen she had three rows of built-in cabinets, one row for each of the children. Each week the school principal sent a list of the supplies and materials for each of the six school days. She would begin a week ahead of time filling the cubby holes. The two boys were very conscientious, but the girl always had a problem getting it all to school on time. Mothers were responsible, and if all was not well, it was the mother who was called in to sit at a desk and hear all her shortcomings.

Before I went to bed I was to take a bath. The mother took me to the bathroom. At the door, the house slippers were taken off, and clogs were put on to accommodate any wetness. Her English was limited, so she demonstrated the procedures for taking a bath. First of all, she gave me a bucket of soapy water and a sponge. I was to wash all over before getting in the tub. The tub was narrow, but very deep, and filled nearly to the top with warm water. As I got in, my large body displaced a lot of water. After my soak, I got out. I was dismayed to see that there was only six inches of water for the members of the family to bathe in. I dried off, put on my night clothes and returned to the living room, where I was to sleep on a pad close to a heater in the center of the room. This heater heated the entire house in the winter months.

Hosted by the Professor of University of Kyoto

He took me on a tour of the city of Kyoto. I was surprised that the professor was over six feet tall, and was very fluent in the English language. He took me to see many Buddhist shrines. He was the former Japanese ambassador to South Korea. He said there was a rumor that Koreans intended to build an automobile. He dismissed the idea that it would ever run; Korean precision engineering was not sufficient to the task. This statement reflected many Japanese feelings of superiority to other Asian national groups. I visited a school district just outside Tokyo that had many Korean children. These were descendants of slaves. The school had a human rights advisor to assure the children were not mistreated. As in Milwaukee, I did not know I would travel so far to find problems so similar to those prevalent in Milwaukee, Wisconsin.

During a snowstorm, I left Tokyo on a bullet train for Yokohama. The train slowed to 180kph due to limited visibility. Once there, I visited many schools. The schools seemed to have a similar look, reminding me of a Holiday Inn. There were no hallways; all passages were outdoor walkways. They also had no centralized heating. In the morning, they would turn the lights on, which would take off some of the chill. The children would wear their outside clothing as necessary. Turning on a space heater was a last option.

Blueprints for Schools for the Handicapped

With 1,700 schools in Tokyo, there was not one school for handicapped children. I told them I was building a replacement school for handicapped children that would include both children of normal abilities and those with multiple handicaps. The Japanese educators were interested, and asked that I send them the blueprints for the school. The school design included two pools, one of which was a therapy pool with provisions for bringing in wheelchair students, and lifts to move them in and out of the pool.

Care of Five Year Olds on Subway

I observed the preschoolers walking down three tiers, unattended, to board the subway to take them to their school. Everyone watched after these children. Each wore a red hat, a backpack with their name, address and the address of their school. Once on the subway, they had a special raised area in the corners to place them above the crowd where they can be seen and protected. Riders make certain the little ones get to the area safely through the throng. These children are on the fast track to University of Tokyo. Some of the kindergartens are actually located within sight of the university. There is good reason to get the child started on this path, since the graduates become staff at the most prestigious government offices, such as the Office of the Treasury, or they join a large industrial firm to reach an upper management position.

Respect for CEOs

I noticed when a CEO of a large firm boarded a train, his immediate staff were there with flowers and other courtesies to see him off. The process was repeated upon his return. This respect for leadership was noted throughout my visit to Japan.

Teachers Go on Strike at High School

The Teachers' Union is nationwide in Japan, but they can go on strike for local issues. I arrived at a high school where teachers were picketing the school from 8:00-8:30 a.m., which was allowed only on their own time.

I asked the principal what issue they were striking against. He replied they did not want the national anthem played at the graduation ceremony; it was too militaristic. Teachers' meetings are held after the children's school day. The principal held a meeting that day. Each teacher had her say. At the end of the meeting he announced they would play the national anthem at the graduation. That settled the strike. That demonstrated the Japanese respect for authority.

Downtown Tokyo

Police, in groups of thirty or forty, gathered on a street corner to get their instructions for the shift. They then dispersed two by two to patrol the various businesses; none of the patrolmen carried weapons.

It was fascinating to see the businesses all open on schedule. There was a ceremony for the opening, with the CEO opening the doors to the public. At each station inside the store there were two uniformed clerks to care for customers. They were constantly busy polishing and arranging any time there was a time free of customers.

I recall no policemen directing traffic. All seemed to flow without congestion or jostling.

Middle School Students Practice Graduation Exercise

At this middle school in Yokohama, the students were in charge of graduation ceremonies. They had a student master of ceremonies, student speakers and musicians. They were to graduate on Friday night with their parents in attendance. They had Saturday school off to celebrate their achievements. On Monday morning they would resume school as usual, having graduated to the next level.

Elementary School Children Conduct Lunch Time Activities

A delegation of children from each class went down to a small kitchen to get all needed for the luncheon meal: a tray of food, silverware and a bottle of milk for each student. This small group served their classmates, who were seated at their desks. The president of the class introduced the guests, and we all went about eating our lunch. I could not get the bottle of milk open. The child next to me popped it open in a flash. After everyone had finished eating and the traces of the meal had been removed, the classroom teacher was introduced to present a lesson on nutrition. The topic of this day's lunch time was milk, and the importance of consuming calcium. With the charts and pictures, the lesson was easy to understand, despite any language barrier.

Each school had domestic animals cared for by the students. They were kept in cages outside the classrooms. Children had total responsibility for their care.

Middle School Children Look Alike

I noticed in the middle school it was difficult to make a gender distinction: they had the same looking backpacks, same hair style, all wore uniforms, and were of a similar size. This was all part of the standardization throughout Japan.

CHAPTER 10

Rich Experiences in Ukraine and with the Ukrainian People

Brother Roger and wife Diane were drawn to Ukraine. Roger was the minister of music at the Coral Ridge Presbyterian Church in Fort Lauderdale, Florida. He was invited by a Unitarian Priest to come to the Ukraine after the Berlin Wall came down and Ukraine became independent. In Roger's first visit to Ukraine he selected the musicians to perform Handel's Messiah. He and his wife came home on separate planes. Both were moved by the experience they had in Kiev, Ukraine. When they got together in Florida they felt the Lord was calling them to become music missionaries to the Ukraine. So they prepared themselves for this missionary experience and left without the missionary board support for Kiev, Ukraine. Upon arrival at the train station, the priest was not there to greet them, so they arranged to take all of the luggage to the curb, and paid a cab driver to take the many suitcases of music and go to a hotel. They begged a cart from a repair man. They paid the cab driver $10 for the fare to the hotel. They were told they could have had a cab driver for an entire month for $10. Without knowing the Russian language, they assembled the musicians to perform The Messiah and other classical works, which had not been allowed for 70 years by the Russians.

Now being retired as a school superintendent, I began giving nearly full time to see that the Music Mission Kiev was founded on a sound footing. He needed an organization to support the mission and I helped put that all together. I soon made a trip to Ukraine by flying first to Moscow and then taking the train to Kiev. In Moscow I was to meet one of Roger's staff members at the airport, but he was confused, since the Russians changed the number of the flight in mid-air. We finally made connections and took the long train ride to Kiev. Upon arriving at the train station in the evening, I found people were sleeping on empty spaces on the floor throughout the train station, which indicated that there were many homeless people coming in from out of the cold.

It Takes Three Keys to Get into Roger's Apartment

Living in a multi-story building with apartments was a rich experience in itself. It took three keys to get into the apartment: one for a gate, another for an all metal fireproof door, and finally a key for the wooden door. All the apartments were very small. The kitchen was so small it would only hold two people. All the kitchens had standard equipment including a small refrigerator, a sink, and a gas stove top burner.

Also, the toilets in a twelve story apartment were stacked one on top of another with the pipes exposed with no seals on them. The odors were transferred from floor to floor. Since all the apartment buildings were alike, I asked Roger how he knew he was in the correct apartment building. He said there were two ways to tell: one was by the repairs that were needed, and the second was

ABOVE: *Kiev, Ukraine apartment building needing only "small" repairs.* LEFT: *Small kitchen in my brother Roger's Ukraine apartment.*

the smell of your apartment building when you got inside. One thing you would notice was that nothing was ever repaired. The sidewalks, benches outside the buildings and the sprinklers were never repaired. One reason you could smell your apartment building was that the garbage chute would fill up to the 12th floor before it was collected.

Results of the Soviet Rule

- When the Soviet government invaded Ukraine, the Ukrainians protested and the Soviets clamped down by killing 12 million people. They did this by starving the Ukrainians and taking away their food. They also executed, one-by-one, 300,000 Ukrainians who had knowledge and expertise in certain areas of government. They buried them one-by-one in a forest without grave markers.

- Jews were required to have special identification; they could not have Russian or Ukraine passports. They were neither Russian nor Ukrainian; they were identified as Jews. This meant that they were not citizens and lacked the privileges of being a citizen because they were Jews.

- Much of the Russian nuclear technology and the missiles sites came from the newly conquered Ukrainians. The missiles were manufactured in the Ukraine, as well as a number of missile sites targeting the US from the Ukraine.

- The Soviets persuaded them that now they were in a workers' paradise. To some this meant they wouldn't have to do hard work anymore. So nothing was repaired. Street lights that were damaged were never fixed, doors that were hanging off the hinges were never repaired, and there was a feeling that you could steal because everything belonged to the people. So if you replaced the lights outside your apartment door, the bulbs would be stolen immediately.

- The Soviets destroyed 1,700 churches in Kiev. They kept a synagogue and made it into a museum to atheism. They kept one Polish built cathedral and made it the museum to the organ.

ABOVE: Monument in forest to 300,000 Ukranians executed by the Soviets.
LEFT: My sister Norma in the forest where Ukranians have posted the names of 300,000 killed by the Soviets.

- Russian became the official language and students were taught only Russian in their schools. The school curriculum was filled with propaganda. When I visited an English language class, the book they were using said that all the rivers and streams in America were polluted. They used the story of a river in Cleveland where a student threw a match into a river and it caught fire.

- Students were selected early in their school careers to become trained as musicians or Olympic stars. In some respects all musicians were property of the government and Roger had to request individually to fill 165 positions in the Kiev Symphony and Chorus.

- Poverty was observed everywhere. In the subways, widows would be selling their kitchenware and even their clothing in order to get money for food. My brother Roger observed the plight of the widows and started a mission for the widows by distributing sacks of groceries to their apartments every week to keep them alive. Teachers, doctors, and other professionals were all paid by the government, and only $20 a month.

- When taking the train from Moscow to Kiev, Ukraine after you left Moscow, you saw no paved roads. At the railroad crossings you could see mud roads filled with deep ruts from trucks and wagons.

- Roger said if you want to see over 1,000 people cry at a music concert, perform one of Tchaikovsky's symphonies, which they weren't allowed to hear for more than seventy years because it carried some Christian themes and was probably ordered by the Czars.

- In Kiev, you could see the results of the Russian motivated

LEFT: *My brother Roger started a mission for widows who had no money to buy food. These people are peeling potatoes in Ukraine to help feed 100 widows.*
RIGHT: *Statue of Mother Russia on the highest hill in Kiev, Ukraine.*

architecture. The Soviets felt that they might become the replacements of the Roman Empire, so they put up buildings with Roman columns, but often the buildings were of poor construction. At Christmas time one year a crowd was outside one of these buildings and the facing of the buildings fell off and killed as many as 100 people. In fact, many of the apartments were made out of pre-manufactured slabs, so if an earthquake would come to this region, the buildings would fall down like a house of cards. Can you imagine living in an apartment with cement slabs overhead which could collapse at any time?

- There was thick mud on the side of buses in Moscow and Kiev. I asked why these vehicles went on the muddy country roads and they said, "No, instead of using salt and cinders in the winter, we use mud."

- The Soviets influence on agriculture was evident in Ukraine where, for the Europeans, they were the bread baskets. The farms were managed by the Soviets and there was hardly enough produce to ship to Europe. Since these policies were such a disaster, the Soviets finally allowed small gardens to be planted, which produced more food than they received from government farms.

- The Soviets managed the heating of the apartments by handbook; therefore, before the heat was turned on it could be as cold as below zero degrees before the date for turning on the heat was reached. Sometimes the apartments were overheated, so much so that the windows on the top floor had to be opened. Nothing seemed to be regulated.

- The Ukrainians told me that the Soviets drafted all of the young men from the Ukraine to take part in the battle against the German invasion during WWII. It was said that the Ukrainians were put on the front line and no more than 10 percent ever returned to Ukraine.

Observing the Missionary Effort

Early on, Roger developed the Kiev Symphony and Chorus, whose concerts were well attended. Many of the tickets were free, but others sold for nickels and dimes.

Roger also had a translator, since he didn't know the Russian language. The translator, who was an atheist, asked him, "Don't you Christians have churches? Don't you read the Bible?" Since the Soviets kept the scripture out of the hands of the Ukrainians, Roger started handing out Bibles with help from the mission funding. He started a church with a membership and developed Bible study groups with the congregation, particularly with the widows. All the Christian hymns were translated into Russian and Roger's musician often provided the music at the Sunday services.

I was invited to stay overnight at the home of a member of the choir Roger directed. I learned that he was captain of a nuclear missile site.

Invited to Stay Overnight at Missile Site Captain's Apartment

I was invited by one of the members of the choir to stay overnight at his home. The apartment only had one bedroom for him and his family. I slept on the davenport and two dogs slept underneath the davenport. At the dinner table I found out that he was captain of a missile site that was targeted on a site in the US. He got out a map and wanted to know where I lived. At that time I had lived close to Cleveland, Ohio. He was happy to know that I wasn't targeted by the missile site. Its target was in New Mexico, but at this time the Ukrainians gave up all their nuclear weapons and missile sites in agreement with the US.

A Birthday Party at the Home of Survivor

When the Germans arrived in Kiev during WWII, they invited 100,000 Jews to a location where they would receive instruction. In the beginning some Ukrainians thought that the Germans would free them from the Soviets, but very early on they found out that the Germans were just as cruel. On separate occasions the Germans opened fire with machine guns and killed 100,000 Jews within minutes. This event was known as Babi Yar. There was a birthday party planned at the home of one of Roger's staff members; he was the chief administrator of the Symphony and Chorus. We were celebrating his son's 18th birthday and his father was still there. His wife had just passed away from breast cancer. He was one of the few survivors of those Jewish massacres. As a twelve-year-old he quickly realized that everybody was going to be killed, so he began to run. He ran and ran until he came to a rural home to seek shelter. He was raised by a Christian family. On another occasion, we visited the family and they took us to the memorial of Babi Yar. It was the ugliest structure you could imagine, with rusted steel beams stacked as high as a two or three story building commemorating the massacre. It got cold that evening and they furnished us winter parkas so we would be warm in our travels back to the apartment.

My Second Visit to Ukraine

At the invitation of the Kiev symphony choir, I returned to Ukraine. They wanted to give a memorial service for Roger's (and my) mother, who had just passed away. Despite being on a very limited fixed income, she had been a loyal supporter of the mission to Kiev, Ukraine for years.

Since I had made the trip before, I knew how to get there. I took my sister Norma and her husband, Don Burris, with me. We first flew to Moscow, Russia, and since they hadn't ever been to Moscow before, we visited Red Square and other sites in Moscow. We then we went to the Kiev railroad station to board a train to Ukraine. It was a long trip. The train had to change the wheels to accommodate the road rails between Russia and Ukraine.

I gave a eulogy for my mother, and the audience was very fascinated by the fact that she was a farmer's daughter and had been

I took my sister Norma and her husband Don to see the Kremlin on our way to Ukraine.

My brother Roger at an open market in Ukraine.

a teacher in a one-room schoolhouse in the state of Iowa. Many hymns and pieces of classical music were performed in honor of Mother McMurrin.

Experiences at the Open Market

I had an opportunity to go to the open markets to shop for the widows. Here I experienced the operation of the Mafia. I saw a man in a large jacket going around the various food displays collecting the weights from the scales if the lady had not paid the fee to the Mafia for protection. There were no sacks or containers for the food; it was sold only by the weight. Thus, the ladies were out of business if they didn't pay their fees.

A man at the market came up to me and said that I was trying to be disguised, but he knew I was an American. "You are the only one with shiny shoes." Shiny shoes seemed to be the trademark of an American.

At the Apartment, Food is Bagged for the Widows

The food bought at the markets was brought to the apartments. A special room was set up to bag up the food, which was then delivered to the widows. There, widows lived alone in these apartments and would starve to death otherwise. One widow said she could not receive the first cut of meat because she had just sold her last pot. Poverty was such that women were reduced to selling their pots and underwear in the subway.

Attending Numerous Concerts

Since the apartments were close to the music hall, we attended many concerts, which was a real treat. On one occasion I met a man who was wearing his army jacket with numerous ribbons and medals displayed across his chest. He was one of the few survivors of the Great War, which was WWII. I had my picture taken with him because he was such an anomaly, being a survivor of the Great War.

I met this man in a music hall. He was a survivor of World War II and wore his military medals and ribbons on his Army jacket.

Unusual Response from Ukrainian Women

My brother Roger had a luncheon table of Ukrainian women engaged in conversations. They wanted to know if Americans lived in apartment houses. He said that most Americans live in individual homes and had two car garages. They wanted to know why you needed a two car garage. He said some Americans have two cars. One woman got mad and stood up and pounded her fist on the table because she thought that the Americans had stolen their cars. Under communism everything was handed out. Everybody had to get one item before they could get two. So for the Americans to have two cars, they must have stolen them.

New Apartment for Office and the Mission

The music mission was so beloved in Ukraine that it found many American supporters. Their support enabled the mission to purchase a far more upscale apartment close to the music hall. This was a much larger apartment which was used by the mission and by Roger's family. Some days after church service, a luncheon was provided at this new facility. The facility was within easy walking distance of the music hall. Roger employed several Ukrainians to administer the office and as well as provide household services.

Cars Parked on Sidewalks

There were very few private cars in Kiev Ukraine, but the cars were close to individual businesses to prevent them from being stolen.

CHAPTER 11

Rich Experiences in Amateur Radio and Technology

At an early age I was very interested in radios and how they worked. Our family owned an Atwater Kent Radio which had many tubes and a separate speaker. Our family listened to the news. During WWII we heard many speeches from President Roosevelt and Winston Churchill. I built a small radio so I could hear short-wave broadcasts on BBC and Radio Moscow. At the age of 14 I built a large superhetradyne radio receiver from the schematic in a handbook published for ham radio operators. I had to wind the plug-in coils to receive the amateur radio bands with many stations on them. My father kept this radio in his possessions as they moved from place to place. In his retirement from the ministry, he wanted to know if he should keep it for me. I told him that I had other radios that were much better. Now I wish I had gone and picked it up because it would be an achievement in radio construction and a relic from the past. That radio would be nearly 70 years old now.

Becoming a Licensed Mature Radio Operator

During WWII I was unable to get licensed to broadcast to amateur radio bands, but in 1988 I was determined to get my own amateur radio license so I could go on the air and make broadcasts around the world. I had to learn Morse code and know all the regulations that were required for all amateur radio operators. Ham radio operators around the world, if you made contact with them and they were motivated enough, would send you contact cards with all the info about the connections. I have 46 of these from different nations, some with Morse code contacts and some with voice contacts. I have made contact with every state, including Hawaii and Alaska.

Setting up an Amateur Radio Station

My first station was a transceiver I bought from Radio Shack that would only use the ten meter band. It's amazing how many stations I contacted on this very limited radio. Later on I upgraded my license so I could work more amateur radio bands and bought a Kenwood 2000, which featured all the amateur radio bands; now I was on the air with 100 watts. Initially my station had wire antennas, but at my home in Shaker Heights, Ohio the amateur radio operator owned the house. He had a large Yagi antenna on a telephone pole close to a giant maple tree. In a spring storm the antenna came down into the tree, and in a second storm the antenna came down to the ground. I saved the parts that were usable and when I moved to Bend, Oregon I brought the parts along so I could put a reconstructed antenna up in my back yard. I had a book on the theory of Yagi antennas written by a missionary to India's son who became an engineer. I took his design for a Yagi directional antenna with the two elements for the 20 meter band. On this station I could get easy access to Eastern Russia and Japan. Sometimes I'd get signals from the South Sea Islands, along with Australia and New Zealand. Later on I used the additional parts to design an antenna for ten meters. This antenna had three elements and, after installing it in my backyard, the first station I had contact with was in the Union of South Africa, which was a surprise to me and to the operator.

Equipping a Second Station in my Winter Home

I now have a winter home in a Seattle suburb where I have equipped another amateur radio station. This station is equipped with a Yeasu 950 transceiver. I've installed two vertical antennas; one is attached to the patio railing and the other is attached to a large fir tree. These antennas are not as good as the Yagis, but I have been able to contact a number of Hams throughout the world. On the West Coast it is easier to get into Asia and into Siberia.

Amateur radio operators have invented a digital system which I have used to get around the world, using only 10 watts of power. It's an amazing system that calls for unique software as well as equipment to connect your computer to take the messages.

CHAPTER 12

Rich Experiences as an American

Background: Universities and Colleges

The United States has a diverse and rich array of colleges and universities, both public and private. As of 2014, there were 7,690 colleges/universities in the US. This resource has assisted students from many backgrounds and economic levels to obtain a post-secondary education. The New York Times reported (June 28, 2014) that, according to a recent ranking by the London-based Times Higher Education, 18 of the world's top 25 universities are American. Similarly, the Academic Ranking of World Universities, published annually by Shanghai Jiao Tong University, gives us 19 of 25. After World War II, the GI Bill (formally known as The Servicemen's Readjustment Act of 1944) provided financial assistance to returning service members, many of whom would not have been able to afford college. Other programs, such as Pell Grants, provide outright grants to low-income and other students to support post-secondary education. These funding programs, and others, have helped to build America's middle class and help citizens achieve economic and professional goals.

I was able to access a church college which was supported over time by the congregations throughout America and the world. I attended Olivet Nazarene College for four years, graduating in 1952 with honors. All of my brothers and my sisters attended this college also, so my family accessed this resource.

After graduating from ONC I immediately enrolled in the University of Cincinnati. It had been built and financed by the City of Cincinnati. Later on it became part of the Ohio University System. However, I had the privilege of going to this university under the G.I. bill, which made it nearly free to me as a veteran of the Korean War. I was a school administrator of a district just outside Columbus, Ohio. I began working on a PhD in educational administration; the school district administration had an agreement with Ohio State University to provide tuition free graduate experience. I took advantage of this privilege and gained a number of credits over the years. Moving to Toledo, Ohio to become the deputy superintendent of schools, I attended the University of Toledo which, again, was built and financed by the City of Toledo, but was now a part of the Ohio University System. I continued to be supported by the G.I. bill of rights, which was very encouraging. Over the years I graduated with a PhD in Administration and Education. Like many Americans, the resource of colleges and universities had been advantageous to its young citizens and I was able to take part in it.

The Railroad System
Background: America's System of Railroads

America's freight railway system is recognized in the industry as the best in the world. Each day, US railroads deliver an average of five million tons of goods and serve almost every industrial, wholesale, retail, and resource-based sector of the economy. Railroad transportation is the most environmentally efficient way to move freight over land. Passenger trains, including transit systems and Amtrak, provide daily transportation for urban commuters and transcontinental travelers. In 2010, passenger rail transport provided 27.6 billion passenger kilometers of transportation.

At age 16 I was now eligible to work on the Chesapeake and Ohio Railroad in Walbridge, Ohio. It was a well-paying job and I served as a clerk and put my paycheck in the bank so I could go to college. Each summer I came back from college to work on the railroad. When the family moved to the Cincinnati area of Ohio, I went to work for the Baltimore and Ohio Railroad in Dayton, Ohio. I had to wake up at 4:30 every morning to get to Dayton by 7:00 a.m. I got excellent pay as a railroad clerk because I was able to take some of the top positions from those who were on summer vacation. But again, I saved my money so I could go back to college. These experiences may seem like ancient times because we had only steam engines; diesel engines came later.

As an employee of the railroad I would get free passes to go to New York City and Washington, DC. In Washington DC I visited many of the historic monuments. The Capitol was within walking distance from the train station. I remember walking there and hearing the Marine Corps band. Of course I visited the Lincoln Memorial and read Lincoln's words carved in stone. It always made me happy. I took a trip alone to New York City and took in the tall buildings and the sights of a major city. I thought the Lincoln Hotel would be the best place to stay overnight. I found out that that wasn't true. In reality, it was a sleazy establishment, but it was cheap.

Background: The Airline System

From those two Dayton Wright brothers' experiments on the beach, a wealth of international, national and regional commercial airlines grew to encompass serving the United States. Since the deregulation of the industry, consolidation has actually stabilized the industry and allowed carriers to update and upgrade passenger services and invest in new technology. In 2011, customer complaints were only 1.18 per 100,000 customers – much lower than other forms of transport. Increases in personal income are outpacing the cost of air travel, so consumers can purchase about 2.5 times they could when deregulation began. Also, many of the high-value consumer goods we enjoy reach the US by air. In 2014, the total of those goods was valued at $986 billion.

As a member of the Large Cities Superintendent Association, I used the airline system quite extensively, attending meetings throughout the US. I visited nearly every major city in America. Most recently, I have used the airports to visit my relatives who are scattered throughout America and the world. I flew several times to Israel and Japan at the invitation of the Ministers of Education of Japan. They put several thousand dollars into buying my ticket on a Japanese airline with a special seat upfront in the Boeing 747.

Background: Government Services

The US form of government has enjoyed a mostly stable and safe environment since its founding more than 200 years ago. The three branches of federal government – legislative, executive and judicial – were designed to provide a system of checks and balances. This system helps to protect the nation from the uprisings and dictatorships experienced by some nations in the world. While the Constitution is the supreme law of the land, each state has the authority to make its own laws as long as they do not contradict the Constitution. Government services, such as issuing licenses, business permits, social welfare programs, and many others, are authorized via the powers of the federal, state and local government. In many cases, legislation is passed to authorize a service and how it is to be delivered. The federal government of the US substantially expanded its services during the Great Depression.

Many of the services instituted in that era, such as Social Security, still exist today.

Very early in your development you learn that we are a government of law and order, but it is broken down into many different systems from local to federal, as well as world governments. I think as a child I realized that local government controlled the use of the car with the necessity of a license, as well as following the laws providing for the system to work and for the safety of the drivers and passengers.

The most recent service I receive from the government, which is very consistent, is my Social Security check.

A Constitution Formed by our Founding Forefathers

In school we learned about the origin of our country and the Declaration of Independence, as well as the Constitution. I learned later that each state also has a constitution. One of these provides the rights for the citizens, which are not always equal, but over time that has been corrected.

Background: Hospitals and Medical Services

The American Hospital Association reports there are 5,686 hospitals registered in its database, offering a total of more than 914,000 hospital beds in the nation. There are more than 661,000 physicians and surgeons in the US, representing a wide range of specialties. Medical students from other countries choose to receive their training in the US due to its established reputation as an excellent environment for instruction, residencies and internship. In the past, access to medical care was difficult for many people. With the advent of Medicare in 1965 and the Affordable Care Act (sometimes called Obamacare) in 2013, more individuals have secured health care coverage.

In my lifetime I have received many services from doctors and hospitals. My first experience was falling off the porch in Evansville, Indiana as a five year old and breaking my arm right at the shoulder. It was set at the hospital, but still tormented me very much with pain, so I returned to the hospital so they could re-break and set the arm. As a seven year old I broke my arm while walking to school. This time I slipped on the ice and broke my elbow. I had complained so often about broken bones that my father hadn't believed me when I said I had broken my arm. When I finally took my jacket off, he saw my arm and took me to the hospital and had it set and cast. In Milwaukee I broke my arm playing basketball, so again I had to use the services of the hospital to have it set and cast. Living in Shaker heights, Ohio I was diagnosed at Mt. Sinai Hospital and told that I needed a bypass surgery for four arteries leading to my heart. This was a wonderful hospital which also gave free service to indigent patients who lived nearby. That practice eventually caused it to go bankrupt. This was a great loss to the community. In Bend, Oregon I had an arthritic left shoulder, which now has a titanium replacement. In Covington, Washington I went to the local hospital and now I have a left hip replacement. In Shaker Heights I fell off a ladder and broke my wrist in seven places. In Mt. Sinai Hospital they had a world renowned hand and wrist surgeon that put it all back together with seven pins and a brace. I was able to gain back the full range of mobility without pain.

Background: Charitable Organizations in the US

Americans have long been a giving and generous people. Charitable organizations, addressing a wide range of social, economic and health issues, are well embedded in our culture. The American Red Cross was founded in 1881. It is the only congressionally mandated organization to provide aid to victims of disaster. The Salvation Army adopted that name in 1878, and continues to serve more than 30 million people in the US each year through its various social programs, making it the second largest US charity. The United Way is the largest charity in the US, and is largely dependent on payroll deductions from American workers. Other leading charities are Feeding America, Goodwill Industries, YWCA and YMCA, American Cancer Society, and St. Jude Children's Research Hospital.

Charitable Organizations Such as Red Cross and Salvation Army

I contribute annually to a whole array of charitable organizations, such as the Red Cross, the Salvation Army, cancer research, Music Mission Kiev, church organizations, American Bible Society, Friends of Israel, and colleges and universities I have attended. With the American Bible Society I have an annuity for my wife who was a faithful contributor and a great Bible student. I also set up another annuity for my brother Dwight, who was a veteran Bible teacher at a Catholic high school in Middletown, Ohio. He was probably the best Bible teacher they ever had. He supported all their athletic contests and when a student would come to him and quote the verse for the week, he would give them extra credit in his grade book. In his retirement they would still come to him at a basketball game and quote scripture. We also got Meals on Wheels because, in my wife's last days after fighting cancer for seven years, we took advantage of this service.

Background: Monuments

The United States has 113 protected areas known as national monuments. The President of the United States can establish a national monument by presidential proclamation, and the United States Congress can by legislation. President Theodore Roosevelt established the first national monument, Devils Tower in Wyoming, on September 24, 1906. Monuments throughout the nation honor milestones in US history, house and protect important artifacts, some dating to prehistoric eras, and provide a way

My grandson Wynston in front of the Capitol building in Washington, DC in 2013. I was pleased to find the building so well kept.

for average citizens to experience and understand historic events and sites. Washington, DC offers the most concentrated access to important monuments, including the White House, Lincoln Memorial, Washington Monument, Korean War and Vietnam War memorials. Thirty states have national monuments, including Mount Rushmore in South Dakota, and the Statue of Liberty in New York City. Arizona has 18 national monuments, the most of any state.

I personally visited the monuments of Washington DC many times and made sure my children, and now my grandchildren, had the opportunity to visit these monuments. In the spring of 2013 I took my daughter and my grandson to Washington DC to visit the monuments.

I was particularly impressed by the Capitol, which was so well kept that there wasn't a scuff on the floor or any damage to the walls. It was in perfect condition. It was a very friendly atmosphere. I was so impressed because it seemed like such a contrast to the attitude of the Congress that didn't want to appropriate money for the repair of our infrastructure. Thus, I was impressed that they at least kept the Capitol of our country in shape, which is to their credit.

On one of my earlier visits to Washington DC, the monument to those who served in the Korean War was a small statue with inscriptions, but on my latest visit the Korean War monument was very extensive. It was an enclosed area with life-sized soldiers on the attack and my grandson was impressed that one soldier carried a radio, as well as his rifle, which was what his grandfather carried in the Korean War. The memorial to the Vietnam soldiers was quite impressive as well. My wife's maiden name was Funderbunk, so we looked up family names on the display and found a Colonel Funderbunk. A search of the internet gave the information that he was a helicopter pilot and was shot down in South Vietnam on one of his rescue missions. That was the only family name that we could find on the display.

The monument to the soldiers who served during the WWII was quite expansive. There was a separate one for the Pacific and another for the European sector. The soldiers were honored state by state. Martin Luther King Junior's monument was very expansive. They had his words on large plaques carved in stone, which centered on the larger than life statue. Of course Lincoln's memorial, with his words engraved in stone, is a memorial to his leadership and saving the nation. The Lincoln Memorial also has the name of every state in the Union, which has its name carved in stone around the monument itself.

Background: National Park System

America's first national park, Yellowstone, was founded in 1872 under the direction of President Ulysses S. Grant. More parks soon followed, and the late 19th century saw cultural sites, such as Arizona's Casa Grande, receiving national designation. President Theodore Roosevelt was one of the parks system's greatest supporters. Five national parks were created during his presidency, as well as 18 national monuments, four national game refuges, 51 bird sanctuaries, and over 100 million acres of national forest. But without a central organization to oversee and protect the parks, private commercial interests began to exploit their resources. As a result of a crusade by a wealthy industrialist, Stephen Mather, the National Park Service was created in 1916. Mather became its first director. His mission was to protect the parks "unimpaired for the enjoyment of future generations," and keep them open for all people. Today, the system includes 392 national parks, monuments, battlefields, seashores, recreation areas, and other areas. Two-thirds of those areas were created to protect historic or cultural resources.

National Forests and Parks

As a young family we took a trip to the Rocky Mountains from Milwaukee, Wisconsin. We used camping equipment to spend each night on the trip in state and national parks. Most often it was free of charge. At Yellowstone National Park, in the month of August, we experienced freezing weather and snow, which was a big surprise. These parks are well kept and their preservation is a tribute to President Theodore Roosevelt. On this trip we visited Mount Rushmore where George Washington, Abraham Lincoln, Theodore Roosevelt, and Thomas Jefferson are immortalized in stone.

Background: Communications

The FCC (Federal Communications Commission) is an independent agency of the US government established by the Communications Act of 1934. It regulates interstate communications by radio, television, wire, satellite, and cable. It does not regulate the print media or internet service providers. Radio includes commercial and public not-for-profit stations, and short wave radio. Satellite radio is not regulated by the FCC. The first television program, a very rudimentary broadcast, hit the US airwaves in the 1920's. However, there were no commercial television sets at that time, so the public was unaware of the technology. This changed in 1927 when Bell Labs and the Department of Commerce (home to the Federal Radio Commission) held the first long-distance transmission of a live picture and voice simultaneously. The television industry we know today was born after World War II. Reginald Fessenden, an employee of Thomas Edison, is credited with transmitting the first radio broadcast in 1906. Before television, radio was the primary means of mass communication. The first radio transmission, consisting of Morse Code, was made from a temporary station set up by Guglielmo Marconi in 1895. Broadcasting music and talk via radio started commercially in 1920-21. Now television and radio programming is even accessible from smart phones. The first commercial telephone services were set up in 1878 and 1879 on both sides of the Atlantic in the cities of New Haven and London. Alexander Graham Bell received his first patent in 1876. Now satellite systems and mobile phones make it possible to connect with almost anyone who has access to this technology.

Communication Systems such as AT&T

As a young child I became familiar with our communication systems through a telephone we had hanging on the wall that tied into a party line which went into a PX exchange. Anybody could listen to your communication on the party line. The lady on the party line would plug you into the party you were trying to reach. In my lifetime I have gone through a series of various upgrades of telephones, even to having a telephone in my car while I was school superintendent in Milwaukee, Wisconsin. One night, coming home from a late board meeting, the phone rang and I had a call from my daughter who was in Phoenix, Arizona. I was one of the first persons to have a car telephone, so this experience was a great surprise to me. I could talk to my daughter late at night as far away as Arizona. AT&T has been a prominent in the organizations and development of wire communications and now they are into the wireless, supporting cell phones. Their investment into research through Bell Labs has brought many inventions into the world of communications. In fact, the first radios I worked with all had vacuum tubes. But Bell Labs invented transistors that took the place of the tubes and made radios more reliable.

Background: Computer Internet and Technology

The story of computers and technological advances in the US is one of individual pioneers and public and private organizations. Bell Labs' invention of the modem in 1958 was one of the first milestones in the creation of the computer internet in the US. In ensuing years, other inventions allowed computers to communicate across time and distance. ARPA (Advanced Research Projects Agency) launched the ARPAnet project, a research program that served as the foundation for today's internet. Email, in its most rudimentary form, was invented in 1972. The term 'internet' was coined in 1974. Fast forward to 1991, when Al Gore created the legislation to fund the "Information Superhighway" and the World Wide Web (WWW) opened to the public. The Mosaic browser, introduced in 1993, helped to popularize the WWW. VoIP—voice over the internet—became a reality in 1996. That same year, email volume surpassed postal mail in the US. Wikipedia was born in

2001. Now the internet and technology are present in almost every aspect of daily life, from reading the morning news to healthcare and its use of advanced medical devices to cell phones and computers that can access seemingly limitless amounts of information on virtually any topic.

In the late 1970s my son and I worked together on advances in technology. At Marshall's urging, after some research we bought our first computer. It was a Corona; it had only one drive, and came at a cost of $2,700.00. The next computer we purchased came with two drives, along with the printer and a smart modem. Now we were able to do word processing, recordkeeping or accounting, and online research.

I was able to get 100 computers donated by IBM for the classroom use of Milwaukee school children. In order to keep up with them I brought one of the computers, loaded with all of the software, home in order to become completely aware of the latest advances in computer technology.

While serving as Deputy Superintendent in Toledo, I served under a very progressive school superintendent. I was to order some books for the new school year. Thus, I looked at the accounting that was furnished to the Board. It showed a large balance in the textbook account, so I went ahead with all the orders so that we could start the school year with books in the hands of children.

The business manager came storming into my office and demanded to know how I could order all those books. I said, "Well, the accounting you gave to the School Board this month showed a good balance in that account, so I ordered the books to start school."

He said, "Do you believe those reports? Come with me to the Accounting Office; then you'll understand that we are three or four months behind in our accounting." There I saw a lady typing in numbers at a machine with large accounting sheets about three feet square. Looking at the stack of purchase orders I could see she was way behind with her duties. The machine look like it was

100 years old, so I reported this to the School Superintendent. We worked diligently to establish a computer center for the school district. In order to accomplish this we had to install a temporary floor and air conditioning in a room for large computers. It was designed around the Chicago computer system, which was supposed to be the best and the latest. In order to keep up with this new world of technology we also installed a public television station for the school system of Ohio, which was eventually dedicated by the Governor of Ohio.

When I arrived in Milwaukee in 1975 as the new School Superintendent, they already had a district-wide computer system and a closed circuit television station. There was also an on-air FM station. Over the years Milwaukee had kept up with the technology. These were tremendous resources when we had to integrate the schools under court order. At that time, the district had 1,700 bus routes.

Early in this process I visited the purchasing department. They were responsible for establishing bus routes and contracting for the buses. I discovered orders sent down there were kept in a shoebox. I knew we were in trouble, so I commissioned the Deputy Superintendent to search for a company nationwide that scheduled trucking firms by computer. He complied very quickly, and through his research found a company headquartered in Beachwood, Ohio that had scheduled several trucking firms by computer. They came to my office to make a presentation, and the district contracted with them to do our scheduling by computer. Each of the 167 schools already had a computer network. They were now able to order the best routes for their new students, the others already being on computer. The principals could search the routes and choose the best route for their student to take. They could also use it for problem solving.

Around this time, I drew upon my own radio experience to work with my son to create our own shortwave radio. In the process he learned technology. By soldering and making those electrical connections, we were then able to make connections worldwide.

With technology ever increasing, my daughters urged me to purchase a cell phone. Now, I am able to keep in daily touch with my family, wherever they may be. The coming of Skype enriches that experience even more, now being able to see them and their surroundings, as well as hear their voices.

Public Libraries
Background: Public Libraries

The public library system in the US is one of the richest sources of information in the nation, and most of these resources are available without charge since they are supported by taxes paid by the citizens of the community. Private philanthropists initially helped to fund public libraries in the US Between 1883 and 1929, Andrew Carnegie financed creation of 1,689 Carnegie Libraries. By 1930, half of all American public libraries had been built by Carnegie. Now it is estimated that there are 119,487 libraries of all kinds in the United States today. Of that total, more than 9,000 are public libraries, and nearly 99,000 are school libraries. The remainder is comprised of academic libraries, special libraries (such as corporate, medical and religious libraries), armed forces libraries and government libraries. As technology has advanced, libraries have expanded their offerings to include e-books, other forms of media, and a wider variety of services.

During the Great Depression, when, as a family, we had very little, we went weekly to the public library, as I recall, in Bedford, Indiana. It was amazing that, in critical economic times, the library was such a rich resource for books, magazines, and newspapers. This was all free to the public and, with a library card, you had access to all of this. In recent times, libraries are now part of every school, every city, every small town and village, and book mobiles are available to households in rural areas. In writing my dissertation I had access to the graduate library, which helped me do my research and complete a 500 page dissertation. The libraries today have a system to assist you in your research where you can get documents from throughout America via existing public libraries.

Restaurants
Background: Restaurants

Today, a restaurant meal is available to almost the entire economic spectrum of the population, and every ethnic and dietary preference. According to the National Restaurant Association, there are one million restaurant locations in the US and 14 million restaurant industry employees. That factors out to about one out of every 10 working Americans. Fully 47% of dollars spent on food are attributed to the restaurant industry. Restaurant industry sales are projected to reach $709.2 billion in 2015. Small wonder that restaurant sales account for four percent of the US gross domestic product. In spite of the number of chain restaurants, most restaurants are still part of the small business economy. Seven in 10 are single-unit operations, and nine in 10 employ fewer than 50 people.

In my childhood during the Depression we almost never went to a restaurant. Once a year my father would take me to a preachers' meeting held in Indianapolis, Indiana where he would allow me to order five cent hamburgers and a milkshake. In my college years, I would try to get a meal for a dollar at a local restaurant. Otherwise, I ate in the cafeteria on campus for ten dollars a week. I very seldom had a date, but if you took a girl out to eat they would sneak some money under the table to help for their share, knowing you were short on money. Also, in the dormitories, it was good to know a GI returned from World War II who always had food.

With my family, we had a tradition of going to a fine restaurant after church on Sundays. You can imagine how many different options we had as far as where to go. To settle this, I usually had to name the restaurant we were going to. It's hard to believe, but you could go to Howard Johnson's to get a fish fry for one dollar each. This was before the one dollar meal advertised at McDonald's. For my children, I would try to find a restaurant or grill where they served old fashioned milkshakes where they gave you a can. Sometimes they couldn't consume the entire milkshake so there was a lot left over for me.

When I retired, we moved to Bend, Oregon. We went to local restaurants so often they knew the wife and me by name. Since she passed away from breast cancer, I have gone back to these restaurants, which have almost become my second home. They know what I am going to order almost before I have sat down at a table. Since moving to my winter home in Seattle, Washington, I frequent local restaurants several times a week.

Law Enforcement and Judicial System
Background: Law Enforcement and Judicial System

The United States is known for having one of the most sophisticated judicial systems in the world. The checks and balances built into the systems allow it to function in a nation as large and diverse as the United States. Law enforcement, courts and corrections are the three major components of the criminal justice system in the US The criminal justice system in the US works differently, depending on the jurisdiction in charge: city, county, state, federal or tribal government or military installation. Most criminal justice systems have five components—law enforcement, prosecution, defense attorneys, courts, and corrections, each playing a key role in the criminal justice process. Throughout the system, constitutional protections exist to ensure that the rights of the accused and convicted are respected, including provisions such as Miranda rights that protect an accused person from self-incrimination and provide an attorney if the accused cannot afford one.

In my childhood I had very few experiences with law enforcement. I recall that in Corydon, Indiana, two police officers brought my brothers home. They had gone to a soda bar and ordered ice cream and couldn't pay for it. In a small town that was easily resolved. Also, I recall that on Halloween night in Walbridge, Ohio my brothers were in the garden throwing tomatoes in the road by our house at the fire engines that were touring the village that night. There was only one policeman in town and he picked up my brothers and took them into town. The mayor called my father and told him to come down, that his boys were there. Again, this was taken care of without any formal charges, which usually happens in small towns.

When I became a chief school administrator in large cities, of course I had more contact with the police department. In Toledo, Ohio the neighbors called the police and told them there was fighting on one of the playgrounds after school. The two policemen got out of their police car to check things out. According to the children's report, one policeman tripped and fell down. Duty officers reported to the police chief that the children pushed the policeman down. Therefore, the police chief decided, when responding to these calls, they should observe from their vehicles so they don't fall down.

Concurrently, the police chief spent thirty minutes instructing the new shift of police protection. This meant there was no protection for school children at three o'clock when school was dismissed. I reported this to the superintendent. We had a high level meeting with the mayor and police chief. I think the mayor was surprised at these reports, but he supported the police chief, I think, because he was new in town. However, the mayor had some choice words for him when they left. At this conference, I mentioned that, since no officers were on duty between three and three-thirty, the school children weren't protected, and also robbers were free to rob the banks between three and three-thirty while briefing was going on. We found that these policies were reversed. We could see the police on the street again.

As school superintendent in Milwaukee, Wisconsin I spent a lot of time in court with our attorneys. I certainly began to appreciate the responsibility of a federal judge and how he conducted the court trial. He found the school district guilty of school segregation, which was unconstitutional. He allowed the superintendent and his staff to come up with a plan to dismantle school segregation and integrate the schools with educational incentives and volunteers. I was impressed that the judge heard from everyone before he rested the case and approved a plan. He even allowed a mentally ill teacher in the Milwaukee public schools, who had been admitted into a mental institution by her parents and had now returned to Milwaukee. At the mental institution, she researched the law and made a complaint which went all the way to the Supreme Court. The Supreme Court ruled that an individual had to consent to being put into an institution. Therefore, many mentally ill patients were released.

CHAPTER 13

Conclusions on a Rich Life

As I look back on my life and the stories in this book, the themes that I remember most and that bring the most joy to my life are those listed below.

1. My mother's influence on a family during difficult times is noteworthy and essential.

2. Rich experiences, of which I am reminded daily, as I listen to news reports.

3. Rich experiences in the family during childhood prepared me for a rich adult life.

4. The work experiences in my youth were a training ground for a career in education administration in difficult times.

5. A talented and creative homemaker as a wife provided a pleasant and comfortable home for her three children and her husband.

6. The joy of good music still lingers in my memory – it was always present in my life.

7. Rich experiences in sports taught me about competition, teamwork and playing by the rules.

8. The experience in the US Army was common to millions of America's young men.

9. Traveling and visiting other countries, mainly Japan, Israel, Russia and Ukraine, has enriched my life tremendously. Making comparisons caused me to appreciate the richness of life we enjoy in the United States of America.

10. My father said he lived during a wonderful period since, on the farm from Iowa, he walked behind a team of oxen, which was common for more than 200 years. And in his later years, he flew on a passenger plane with jet engines.

11. In my experience in the area of communications, I recall our first telephone was mounted on the wall and was connected by wire to a party line. Now, almost daily, I can talk to radio operators around the world through an amateur radio station wireless with very low power using advanced digital technology. Because of advancing technology, I can now talk with brother Roger in Ukraine using no wires, just a cell phone.

Index to Photos

3	My parents, Albert and Myrtle McMurrin
3	My grandfather, Nathaniel McMurrin
3	My grandmother, Mary McMurrin
3	My maternal grandparents, the Brickleys
4	The Antioch church where my parents met
4	The one-room schoolhouse where my mother taught
6	My sister Norma, age 3, and me, age 2
7	My mother with four of her children after surviving the 1937 Johnstown flood
9	The bicycle I received for Christmas when I was nine years old
11	My brother Paul with me on the beach at Pensacola, Florida
20	My lovely wife, Frances McMurrin
23	The home we purchased in Milwaukee from the Case family
23	Frances' talent in decorating a bedroom in our home in Milwaukee, Wisconsin
32	In full uniform at Camp Rucker, Alabama
36	Official portrait as a private first class, Third Infantry Division, US Army
40	Shaker Heights home before exterior restoration
40	Shaker Heights home after exterior restoration
43	Jewish children doing exercises at school
43	Children lining up at a school in Israel
43	Jewish school students armed with weapons
45	Sculpture of the Downtrodden at the Holocaust Museum, Israel
45	Statue of Warsaw Warriors at entrance to the Holocaust Museum, Israel
45	The Wailing Wall in the old quarter of East Jerusalem
45	Jewish soldiers guarding the gate to the Dome of the Rock in Jerusalem
47	Golda Meir Nursery School in Israel
50	A birthday party in the home of the administrator of the Ukraine Symphony Orchestra
50	Monument in Ukraine in memory of 100,000 Jews murdered by the Nazis
63	Kiev, Ukraine apartment building
63	Small kitchen in my brother Roger's Ukraine apartment
65	Monument in forest to 300,000 Ukrainians executed by the Soviets
65	My sister Norma in forest where Ukrainians were killed
67	Peeling potatoes in Ukraine to feed 100 widows

67 Statue of Mother Russia in Kiev, Ukraine
69 Captain of a nuclear missile site, and his wife, in Ukraine
71 My sister Norma and her husband in front of the Kremlin in Russia
72 My brother Roger at an open market in Ukraine
73 World War II survivor in Ukraine
86 My grandson Wynston in front of the Capitol building in Washington, DC

www.ingramcontent.com/pod-product-compliance
Lightning Source LLC
Chambersburg PA
CBHW062102290426
44110CB00022B/2685